Michigan Bucket List Adventure Guide

Explore 100 Offbeat
Destinations You Must Visit!

Sean Holmes

Bridge Press
support@bridgepress.org

Please consider writing a review!
Just visit: purplelink.org/review

ISBN: 978-1-955149-47-1

FREE BONUS

Find Out 31 Incredible Places You Can
Visit Next! Just Go to:

purplelink.org/travel

Table of Contents

How to Use This Book

Welcome to your very own adventure guide to exploring the many wonders of the state of Michigan. Not only does this book layout the most wonderful places to visit and sights to see in the vast state, but it provides driving directions and GPS coordinates for Google Maps to make exploring that much easier.

Adventure Guide
Sorted by region, this guide offers over 100 amazing wonders found in Michigan for you to go see and explore. These can be visited in any order, and this book will help keep track of where you've been and where to look forward to going next. Each portion describes the area or place, what to look for, how to get there, and what you may need to bring along.

GPS Coordinates
As you can imagine, not all of the locations in this book have a physical address. Fortunately, some of our listed wonders are either located within a National Park or Reserve, or are near a city, town, or place of business. For those that are not associated with a specific location, it is easiest to map it using GPS coordinates.

Luckily, Google has a system of codes that converts the coordinates into pin drop locations that Google Maps is able to interpret and navigate.

Each adventure in this guide will include both the GPS coordinates along with general directions on how to find the location.

It is important that you are prepared for poor cell signals. It is recommended to route your location and ensure that the directions are accessible offline. Depending on your device and the distance of some locations, you may need to travel with a backup battery source.

About Michigan

Michigan is the largest state east of the Mississippi River, with an area of nearly 97,000 square miles. It is also the country's tenth most populated state as of the 2020 Census, with a population of nearly 10 million.

The name *Michigan* comes from a version of the Ojibwe word for "large lake." The land was once occupied by various tribes, including the Ojibwe, Ottawa, and Potawatomi tribes, each part of the Council of Three Fires alliance.

French explorers first roamed the land in the seventeenth century. A French fort was established in present-day Detroit in 1701. The land was passed to the British later in the century, and the United States captured it during the War of 1812.

The Michigan territory expanded to a second peninsula to the north in 1835, following an unsuccessful attempt to acquire a strip of land moving through Ohio for use as a canal. Michigan would soon become the country's twenty-sixth state on January 26, 1837.

Michigan has grown in prominence over the years, becoming a critical manufacturing hub. The state remains an essential part of the automotive industry, with the Detroit area housing many automotive manufacturing plants.

Landscape and Climate

Michigan consists of two separate peninsulas. The Upper and Lower peninsulas are separated by the Strait of Mackinac.

The Lower Peninsula features many of Michigan's most prominent cities, including Detroit, Grand Rapids, Saginaw, Ann Arbor, and Battle Creek. The Detroit and St. Clair rivers separate the eastern end of the peninsula from Ontario. The northern part of this peninsula is more forested and includes some of the area's largest inland lakes. The Lower Peninsula also contains multiple moraines formed in former glacial areas, plus sand dunes near the Great Lakes.

The Upper Peninsula features about 3 percent of the state's population. This peninsula is mostly forested by the Hiawatha and Ottawa national forests. The western end contains various mountains, including parts of the Porcupine Mountains.

Four of the five Great Lakes surround Michigan, with Lake Ontario being the exception.

Most parts of Michigan have a warm-summer humid continental climate, although parts of the south have a hot-summer humid continental climate.

Temperatures in the southern part of the Lower Peninsula can exceed 90°F during the summer and can drop to near 0°F in the winter. You can expect about 30 to 40 inches of rain and 50 to 80 inches of snow in this area during the year.

The winter season is more intense in the northern Lower Peninsula and the entire Upper Peninsula. While temperatures can get near 90°F in the summer, they can get down to -10°F in the winter. These areas also experience at least 100 inches of snow from November to April.

Michigan shares borders with Ohio, Indiana, and Wisconsin. Some parts of the southwestern Lower Peninsula are within 100 miles of Chicago.

Michigan has four border crossings that lead to the Canadian province of Ontario. The Ambassador Bridge and Detroit–Windsor Tunnel are two of the busiest crossings between the two countries. There are also crossings in Port Huron and Sault Ste. Marie.

Most of Michigan falls within the Eastern time zone. Four counties in the western end of the Upper Peninsula are in the Central time zone.

Ann Arbor Hands-On Museum

You will find more than 200 science exhibits at the Ann Arbor Hands-On Museum. The venue features various exhibits on the human body, complex machines, and how rockets propel themselves in the air. The museum also has a re-creation of a 1930s country store. Visitors can hold magnets and see how they conduct enough force to attach to items. They can also learn how refraction bends light and changes the way that images look as part of an interactive exhibit.

Best Time to Visit: The museum is open mornings and afternoons from Tuesday to Sunday. The museum also holds occasional special events depending on the season.

Pass/Permit/Fees: Tickets are $16.

Closest City or Town: Ann Arbor

How to Get There: The museum is in the central part of downtown Ann Arbor off of East Huron Street. Take the Jackson Avenue exit off of I-94 to the west. Go east, eventually merging into Huron Street. Keep going east, and you'll find the museum across from the Justice Center. TheRide bus routes 3, 4, and 65 all stop near the museum.

GPS Coordinates: 42.28176° N, 83.74640° W

Did You Know? Part of the museum is housed inside an 1882 fire station.

Bird Hills Nature Area

The Bird Hills Nature Area features 160 acres of land in northern Ann Arbor. You will find sugar maple, dogwood, beech, and oak trees throughout the area. You will also notice old concrete tracks belonging to a farm that was once on the site.

There are five trails to traverse, each an easy few miles in length.

Best Time to Visit: The nature area opens at 6 a.m. Visit early, if possible, as you'll get a beautiful look at the sunrise from here.

Pass/Permit/Fees: You can visit the area for free, but biking is not allowed. Biking could contribute to erosion in the area, possibly harming the land.

Closest City or Town: Ann Arbor

How to Get There: The nature area is north of M-14 in northern Ann Arbor. You can reach the area from downtown Ann Arbor by taking Miller Avenue west and then going north on Newport Road. The nature area is to the right. You can enter through the southwest, or you can continue north and go right on Bird Road to the northeastern entrance.

GPS Coordinates: 42.30119° N, 83.75972° W

Did You Know? Many of the trees around the park were planted in the early twentieth century to produce a more diverse environment in the Ann Arbor area.

Border-to-Border Trail

The Border-to-Border Trail is about 35 miles long and goes from Dexter Township in Livingston County to Ypsilanti Township in Wayne County. The trail goes through multiple townships in the area, with the city of Ann Arbor as the largest place along the path. Much of the path goes alongside the Huron River.

The trail is a unique urban path that passes through many grasslands and local communities. You can take a jog down the road or bike down the extensive two-lane path. The trail is mostly paved, making it easy for you to traverse.

Best Time to Visit: Visit during the morning for great sunrise views.

Pass/Permit/Fees: You can enter the trail from anywhere for free.

Closest City or Town: Ann Arbor

How to Get There: The easiest entry point to the trail is at the St. Joseph Mercy Hospital in Ann Arbor near US-23. The trail is on the western end of the hospital campus near Washtenaw Community College. Most of the trail is also north of I-94.

GPS Coordinates: 42.26555° N, 83.65996° W

Did You Know? Some of the communities in the trail's path are charter townships. A township in Michigan is an organized government with a home rule charter. The Ypsilanti Charter Township is different from the City of Ypsilanti, for example.

Burton Memorial Tower

The Burton Memorial Tower is a landmark building on the University of Michigan campus in Ann Arbor. The 1936 tower is a carillon with 53 bells that stands about 192 feet tall. You'll notice a traditional analog clock at the top end of the tower.

The tower houses some classrooms for the university's school of music. It also features offices for the department of musicology.

The bottom part of the tower has LED lights that allow the tower to shine in many colors. It is often lit in the school's maize and blue colors.

Best Time to Visit: You'll hear the "Westminster Quarters" every quarter hour at the tower.

Pass/Permit/Fees: You can reach the tower for free, but don't expect to get inside the building unless you're a student or you work on the campus.

Closest City or Town: Ann Arbor

How to Get There: The tower is on the northern end of the U of M campus. Take Thayer Street north from University Avenue to reach the tower.

GPS Coordinates: 42.27970° N, 83.73882° W

Did You Know? The carillon at the top weighs about 43 tons, making it one of the heaviest in the world.

Domino's Farms Petting Farm

The petting farm at Domino's Farms in Ann Arbor is a non-profit attraction that teaches visitors about the state's agricultural industry and the value of animals found at farms throughout Michigan. You will find various animals here, including cattle, alpacas, goats, rabbits, sheep, pigs, and chickens.

Visitors can pet many of the animals and learn how to feed them.

Best Time to Visit: The farm offers extended hours on the first Friday of each month. Tractor rides are available during certain times, and food trucks will appear on occasion.

Pass/Permit/Fees: General admission is $6 per person. It costs $2 for each animal feed bag, and a tractor ride costs $2.

Closest City or Town: Ann Arbor

How to Get There: The farm is 5 miles northeast of downtown Ann Arbor. Take the Plymouth Road exit off of US-23 and go east, turning left on Earhart Road near the East Medical Campus. Go right on Barnyard Bend to reach the farm.

GPS Coordinates: 42.32251° N, 83.67993° W

Did You Know? The farm has an extensive horse stable. You'll find several horses of varying ages at the farm.

Furstenberg Nature Area

The Furstenberg Nature Area in Ann Arbor is a wetlands area on the Huron River. The 38-acre park features a half-mile loop trail and a separate granular trail that goes through the woods and local prairie. A wetland boardwalk connects to some of the most picturesque scenes in the Ann Arbor area. You will find many forms of wildlife while going through the nature area. There are several species of frogs that appear in the spring and summer, while trumpeter swans will appear in the winter before moving to other ponds for spring nesting. You'll also find various birds near the lagoon to the east.

Best Time to Visit: You will see most of the wildlife around here during the spring season. These include painted turtles, frogs, and other hibernating animals.

Pass/Permit/Fees: You can visit the area for free.

Closest City or Town: Ann Arbor

How to Get There: The park is south of the University of Michigan North Campus. Take the Huron Parkway south from the campus and then go right on Fuller Avenue to reach the nature area. You can also reach the area from downtown Ann Arbor by going north on Glen Avenue from Huron Street. The road will soon become Fuller Avenue, which will go east and then to the south.

GPS Coordinates: 42.28060° N, 83.70809° W

Did You Know? The area is subject to controlled burns throughout the year to prevent invasive shrubs and growths from developing.

Graffiti Alley

Graffiti Alley is a graffiti art wall on East Liberty Street in Ann Arbor. The wall features various works of graffiti from local artists. People are welcome to produce their own projects on the walls.

The alley displays many pieces of work that can change throughout the year. These include text sprays, animal portraits, and other distinct designs. The area is considered to be a relaxing and creative spot in the heart of Ann Arbor.

Best Time to Visit: The alley is most active during the University of Michigan school year.

Pass/Permit/Fees: The alley is free to visit.

Closest City or Town: Ann Arbor

How to Get There: Graffiti Alley is on East Liberty Street and is directly west of the Michigan Theater. It is on the northern part of the street. The street is accessible from the University of Michigan campus by going north on State Street and then turning left on Liberty Street. TheRide bus route 23 also has a station to the north on Washington Street.

GPS Coordinates: 42.27955° N, 83.74245° W

Did You Know? The area has been a popular site for graffiti since at least 1999. It becomes crowded enough that sometimes the walls are painted over to create a new canvas.

Hill Auditorium

Hill Auditorium is a performance venue on the University of Michigan campus in Ann Arbor. It opened in 1913 and has seating for about 3,500 patrons.

The auditorium features a megaphone-shaped design inspired by the Mormon Tabernacle in Salt Lake City, including three tiers of seating, each with a unique look.

The auditorium is the home of the Ann Arbor Symphony Orchestra and many ensembles from the University of Michigan School of Music.

Best Time to Visit: The schedule of events will vary, so check the website to see what is coming to the venue.

Pass/Permit/Fees: The ticket prices will vary depending on the shows you attend.

Closest City or Town: Ann Arbor

How to Get There: The Hill Auditorium is in the northwestern part of the U of M campus. It is on North University Avenue across from Ingalls Mall. The Modern Language Building is to the north. University Avenue is accessible from Geddes Avenue to the east. TheRide bus route 23 also stops near the auditorium.

GPS Coordinates: 42.27910° N, 83.73929° W

Did You Know? The Vienna Philharmonic and Berlin Philharmonic are among the touring groups to have played at the Hill Auditorium in the past.

14

Kelsey Museum of Archaeology

The Kelsey Museum of Archaeology is on the University of Michigan campus in Ann Arbor. The museum features thousands of ancient artifacts from the Near East and Mediterranean. It also houses one of the largest collections of items from Egypt outside of Cairo, with nearly 40,000 items having been gathered from the ancient town of Karanis.

Other things at the museum include a collection of mummy masks, Parthian pottery items from the Middle East, and thousands of ancient coins. There is also a near-complete copy of *Description de l'Egypte* from Napoleon's Egyptian campaign on display at the museum.

Best Time to Visit: The museum hosts many special exhibits throughout the year. You can see what is happening by visiting the website.

Pass/Permit/Fees: This museum is free to visit.

Closest City or Town: Ann Arbor

How to Get There: The museum is on State Street on the U of M campus. Take the State Street exit north from I-94, and continue going north on the road until you reach the campus.

GPS Coordinates: 42.27670° N, 83.74102° W

Did You Know? People from the museum have been completing fieldwork projects around the world for nearly 80 years. Some of these projects have been completed in Libya, Italy, Israel, and Armenia.

Kerrytown

The Kerrytown historic district of Ann Arbor is home to the many noteworthy historic sites in the city, including the Ann Arbor Hands-On Museum and the Ann Arbor Farmers Market. The original Zingerman's Deli location is also in Kerrytown.

Kerrytown is noted for having one of the largest LGBTQIA+ communities in the state. The district hosts the annual Ann Arbor Pride Parade every June.

Best Time to Visit: Kerrytown hosts a local business-promotion event on the first Friday of every month. The promotion encourages people to visit some of the many popular businesses in the area.

Pass/Permit/Fees: You can get here for free, although it costs money to dine or buy things at any of the stores.

Closest City or Town: Ann Arbor

How to Get There: Kerrytown goes from Depot Street in the north to Huron Street down south. You can get here from I-94 by taking the Huron Street exit and going east on the road. The Ann Arbor station on the Amtrak Wolverine line is to the north.

GPS Coordinates: 42.28610° N, 83.74536° W

Did You Know? Kerrytown takes its name from County Kerry, a county in northeastern Ireland.

Lillie Park

Lillie Park in Ann Arbor is a park space that features a small lake plus two ponds. You'll find a boardwalk that leads to many of the water spaces. There are also a few limestone trails that will bring you closer to the water, with one trail featuring a small bridge over the lake.

The park includes a playground area and a few athletic fields for soccer, lacrosse, and other field sports. The park also houses the Lloyd and Mabel Johnson Preserve to the south. The area features many forested areas and natural growth.

Best Time to Visit: The features around the park are open throughout the summer months.

Pass/Permit/Fees: The park is free to visit.

Closest City or Town: Ann Arbor

How to Get There: The park is in the southeastern end of Ann Arbor near the Mitchell neighborhood. You can take I-94 west from downtown Detroit and then take Exit 180A to US-23. Go south and then right on US-12. Go right on Platt Road to reach the park.

GPS Coordinates: 42.22399° N, 83.69811° W

Did You Know? The park has a grill that is open for cooking and public events. You'll still have to bring your own charcoal and equipment if you want to use the grill.

Matthaei Botanical Gardens and Nichols Arboretum

The University of Michigan operates the Matthaei Botanical Gardens and Nichols Arboretum. The venue houses a 10,000-square-foot conservatory and multiple walking trails. You will find a reproduction of a Tudor-era garden at the Alexandra Hicks Herb Knot Garden. The garden focuses on healing plants, including various herbs that have long been used for medicinal and cooking purposes. Other features around the venue include a children's garden, a labyrinth, and a collection of native trees.

Best Time to Visit: The perennial garden is highly popular during the spring and summer seasons.

Pass/Permit/Fees: Admission is free, but the daily maximum parking rate here is $5 per vehicle.

Closest City or Town: Ann Arbor

How to Get There: You'll find the gardens about 6 miles northeast of Ann Arbor. Take Division Street north from downtown Ann Arbor, which soon becomes Broadway Street and then Plymouth Road after you cross the Huron River. You'll go through the U of M North Campus while on the road. Turn right on Dixboro Road to reach the gardens.

GPS Coordinates: 42.30210° N, 83.66318° W

Did You Know? One of the five trails is made for children. It's common to find small animal tracks around the trail.

Michigan Stadium

With a capacity of 107,601 people, Michigan Stadium on the University of Michigan campus in Ann Arbor is the world's third-largest sports venue. The venue has been the home to the Michigan Wolverines college football team since 1927. Michigan Stadium has expanded in size over the years, as it was first capable of fitting 72,000 people when it opened. The footings for its foundation were designed to support future expansion efforts in the hope that the venue could fit 150,000 people someday. Michigan Stadium hosts the university's graduation ceremonies as well as ice hockey, soccer, lacrosse, and field hockey events.

Best Time to Visit: You can request a tour at any time of the year. The tour offers a look at the stadium's field, the locker room, and the press box.

Pass/Permit/Fees: Tours are $25 per person. At least five people must take part in the tour.

Closest City or Town: Ann Arbor

How to Get There: The stadium is southwest of the main U of M campus. From the west, take the Jackson Avenue exit off of I-94, then go east on the road. Turn right on Stadium Boulevard. From the east, take the Washtenaw Avenue exit off of US-23 and go west, taking Stadium Boulevard on the left side of the fork.

GPS Coordinates: 42.26598° N, 83.74856° W

Did You Know? The attendance record at the stadium is 115,109, which was set in 2013.

Michigan Theater

The Michigan Theater is a classic movie palace in Ann Arbor that continues to host movie showings. The theater opened in 1928 as a vaudeville stage.

The lobby and auditorium feature many of the original accents in the theater's construction. You'll see a barrel-vaulted ceiling and wrought-iron accents all around.

The 1927 Barton pipe organ is the most popular part of the theater. You can hear the pipe organ being played before film screenings. Plus, it provides musical accompaniment when the theater airs silent films.

Best Time to Visit: The theater hosts various film festivals and concerts throughout the year. Visit the theater's website to see the latest schedule.

Pass/Permit/Fees: Theater admission is $10.50 per person. Ticket prices for concerts will vary by event.

Closest City or Town: Ann Arbor

How to Get There: The theater is on Liberty Street a few blocks east of the University of Michigan campus. The area is accessible from I-94 by taking the State Street exit north, eventually turning left.

GPS Coordinates: 42.27955° N, 83.74176° W

Did You Know? The Barton organ in the theater is one of only a dozen still in its original location. There were nearly 7,000 pipe organs built in the 1910s and 1920s.

University of Michigan Museum of Natural History

The Museum of Natural History on the University of Michigan campus hosts many exhibits delving into the evolution of the land around Michigan. You will find exhibits on the geological formations found throughout the state and how life has evolved for billions of years.

The museum has taxidermy specimens and many artifacts from various human cultures. You will also discover the world of prehistoric life, with many fossils and layouts of dinosaurs and other extinct mammals on display.

Best Time to Visit: The museum is easier to reach during the summer when students aren't as prevalent on the U of M campus.

Pass/Permit/Fees: Admission is free, but the university encourages donations if possible.

Closest City or Town: Ann Arbor

How to Get There: The museum is in the Biological Sciences Building on the U of M campus. Take Geddes Avenue from the east to reach University Avenue, or take Huron Street from the west and go south on Washtenaw Avenue. From there, go right on University Avenue.

GPS Coordinates: 42.27913° N, 83.73447° W

Did You Know? You'll find a mastodon trackway at the museum. The trackway illustrates an approximate look at how a mastodon might have moved in the wild.

Inspiration Point

The town of Arcadia is home to a beautiful lookout spot over Lake Michigan called Inspiration Point. The overlook off of M-22 is accessible from a 370-foot climb up a staircase to the lookout.

The point is near the Arcadia Dunes Baldy Trailhead to the north. You'll see many native trees. Plus, you'll find a small shore area near the end of the water. But the best part of looking out from Inspiration Point is watching the clear blue water of Lake Michigan.

Best Time to Visit: The winter season is an amazing time when the area is covered in white and the water is mostly undisturbed.

Pass/Permit/Fees: You can get to the lookout area for free.

Closest City or Town: Arcadia

How to Get There: The point is on M-22 slightly north of downtown Arcadia. You can reach M-22 from US-31 by going north on US-31 from Manistee and then left on Orchard Highway, which becomes M-22. The point is about 25 miles north of Manistee.

GPS Coordinates: 44.51988° N, 86.23244° W

Did You Know? You can see about 20 miles out from the point on a clear day.

Legoland Discovery Center

The Legoland Discovery Center is an amusement center inside the Great Lakes Crossing Outlets shopping center in Auburn Hills. The center is a kid-friendly venue that features a four-dimensional cinema, laser ride, and an interactive Detroit landscape made with more than 1 million Lego bricks.

A Lego factory tour is offered where people can learn how Lego bricks are built and how different designs are planned. Kids can also attempt to build Lego towers and see if they can withstand a simulated earthquake.

Best Time to Visit: The venue is open year round, but it is especially popular on weekends.

Pass/Permit/Fees: Tickets are $25 per person, but you can get a discount if you order online.

Closest City or Town: Auburn Hills

How to Get There: The Legoland Discovery Center is in the southeastern end of the Great Lakes Crossing Outlets center. You can reach the center off of I-75 by taking the Baldwin Road exit and going south on the road.

GPS Coordinates: 42.70279° N, 83.29584° W

Did You Know? The center is one of many Legoland Discovery Centers found throughout the United States. There are also centers in Atlanta, Philadelphia, Phoenix, and a few other cities around the country.

Mount Bohemia

The Keweenaw Peninsula in the far northern reach of the state's Upper Peninsula is home to the Mount Bohemia skiing area. The mountain region features nearly 100 skiing runs over more than 500 acres of land. The longest is close to a mile long.

Mount Bohemia is open for skiing during the winter, although its paths are mostly diamond rated and not for beginners. The mountain relies on natural snowfall instead of producing snow itself.

The resort also has a Norwegian-inspired spa with exposure to hot and cold water followed by relaxation. The process provides a comforting experience that restores the body.

Best Time to Visit: The skiing season lasts from January to March in most situations.

Pass/Permit/Fees: Daily lift tickets are $80 per person. Ski rentals are available, but the prices will vary by selection.

Closest City or Town: Bete Grise

How to Get There: Take US-41 north from L'Anse, then take a right on Gay Lac La Belle Road when you reach the area. You will find the resort to the left.

GPS Coordinates: 47.39189° N, 88.01327° W

Did You Know? The area around the resort can get 250-300 inches of snow a year.

Beaver Island

You will find Beaver Island about 30 miles northwest of the town of Charlevoix at the northern part of Lake Michigan. Beaver Island hosts a vast Irish community, as many of the residents come from families that immigrated to the island more than 100 years ago. The island features various trails, cottages, and a beach. There are also camping sites on the northern end. The north features a functioning lighthouse, while the south has an inactive 1858 lighthouse.

Best Time to Visit: It is easier to access the island from April to September. Most services that bring people here are closed from January to March.

Pass/Permit/Fees: The ferry costs $30 each way for adults and $20 for children. It also costs $12 each way to bring a bicycle on board. You can also bring a vehicle here, but it will cost at least $100 each way to do that.

Closest City or Town: Charlevoix

How to Get There: Take a ferry or plane ride from Charlevoix to the island. Charlevoix is accessible off of US-31, which goes north from Traverse City and south from Mackinaw City.

GPS Coordinates: 45.75031° N, 85.52582° W

Did You Know? Beaver Island was home to an extensive Mormon community in the 1850s, formed by James Strang after disputes over the LDS movement following Joseph Smith's death.

Fisherman's Island State Park

Fisherman's Island State Park is south of Charlevoix on the northeastern Lake Michigan shore. The park takes its name from Fisherman Island, a small island about 1,000 feet from the mainland.

Fisherman Island is accessible by boat, but sometimes people can walk to the island on the tombolo that is formed when the lake levels get low enough. You'll find various forest spaces and a few small beach spots on the island.

There are about 3 miles of hiking trails around the park. Most of the beaches there are also open for swimming.

Best Time to Visit: The tombolo between the mainland and the island is more likely to appear during the summer months.

Pass/Permit/Fees: The park is free to visit.

Closest City or Town: Charlevoix

How to Get There: The park is 6 miles south of Charlevoix. Take US-31 from Charlevoix to reach the park. US-31 goes through Muskegon, Traverse City, and Mackinaw City, giving you enough places to start your trek.

GPS Coordinates: 45.30685° N, 85.30965° W

Did You Know? The maple and birch trees are the most prominent that you will find in the forest.

Cheboygan State Park Beach

You will find the Cheboygan State Park Beach in the northern part of Cheboygan State Park. The beach is in a park featuring 1,250 acres of land surrounding Lake Huron. You can enjoy swimming in the water or fishing on nearby Duncan Bay.

A few small trails surrounding the beach are open for mountain biking and cross-country skiing.

You can see the Fourteen Foot Shoal Lighthouse in the middle of the water. You can also view the remnants of the defunct Cheboygan Point Light from the beach.

Best Time to Visit: The summer season is a more temperate time for visiting the beach.

Pass/Permit/Fees: The park is free to access, but it costs extra to reserve a camping site.

Closest City or Town: Cheboygan

How to Get There: Take Exit 326 from I-75, then go east into Cheboygan on US-23. Continue going east past the town for 3 miles, and you will find the park entrance to the left.

GPS Coordinates: 45.64669° N, 84.41142° W

Did You Know? The Fourteen Foot Shoal Lighthouse gets its name from the depth of the water, which is much less than what boaters would find in other parts of Lake Huron.

Bare Bluff

Bare Bluff is nearly 600 feet high and appears on the southern shore of the Keweenaw Peninsula, a space on the northern end of Michigan's Upper Peninsula. Bare Bluff is home to the Grinnell Nature Sanctuary, where you can see a 180-degree view of Manitou Island and Lake Superior. You can climb to the top of the bluff, which is about 300 feet high. The lower levels still provide outstanding views of the lake and local surroundings.

Best Time to Visit: You can find various migrating birds here during the fall season. The drafts of warm air from the bluffs provide comfortable spaces for these birds.

Pass/Permit/Fees: The bluff is free to visit.

Closest City or Town: Copper Harbor

How to Get There: Take US-41 North toward the Copper Harbor area. Go right on Gay Lac La Belle Road, then continue on Belle Gris Road after passing the town of Lac La Belle. Go left on Smith's Fisheries Road in Belle Gris, and continue all the way to the sanctuary.

GPS Coordinates: 47.39739° N, 87.91170° W

Did You Know? The Montreal River is to the east of the bluff. The river produces the waterfall as it flows south into Lake Superior.

Brockway Mountain

Brockway Mountain is near Copper Harbor in Michigan's Upper Peninsula. The mountain goes up to about 1,300 feet above sea level. It reaches nearly 700 feet above Lake Superior, providing outstanding views of the town, lake, and nearest forested area.

Brockway Mountain is on the eastern end of Brockway Mountain Drive, a 9-mile scenic road that leads to Eagle Harbor to the west.

Best Time to Visit: Visit in September or October, as the fall foliage season will kick into full gear around this point. Avoid during the winter, if possible, as the area is closed off to vehicular travel during that season.

Pass/Permit/Fees: The area is free to visit.

Closest City or Town: Copper Harbor

How to Get There: You can reach the mountain by taking US-41 north to Copper Harbor from Marquette. Take M-26 west when you reach Copper Harbor, then merge left on Brockway Mountain Drive to reach the peak. You will find the main lookout on the second curve on the road.

GPS Coordinates: 47.46596° N, 87.91140° W

Did You Know? You can see Isle Royale from the top of the mountain on a clear day. It's about 50 miles away.

Estivant Pines Nature Sanctuary

The Estivant Pines Nature Sanctuary is south of Copper Harbor in Michigan's Upper Peninsula. The sanctuary is named for the white pine trees scattered around the area. Many of these trees are more than 120 feet tall and are at least 300 years old. You'll also find balsam fir and sugar maple trees throughout the two hiking trail paths at the sanctuary.

Various birds are present throughout the sanctuary, including hawks and woodpeckers. Nearly 100 bird species have been catalogued at this location.

Best Time to Visit: The summer season is the best time to visit, as winter conditions may be too rough.

Pass/Permit/Fees: The sanctuary is free to visit.

Closest City or Town: Copper Harbor

How to Get There: The sanctuary is accessible from US-41 North. Take US-41 North from Marquette or L'Anse, then take a right on Golf Course Road. You'll then take another right on Burma Road almost immediately after getting on Golf Course Road. The sanctuary is about 150 miles from Marquette or 80 miles from L'Anse.

GPS Coordinates: 47.44230° N, 87.87872° W

Did You Know? You'll find various native wildflowers throughout the landscape, including baneberry and violet. They grow well around the area despite the soil being rather thin.

Hunter's Point Park

You will see Lake Superior from the ends of Hunter's Point Park in the Upper Peninsula. The park is about 9 acres in size and offers views of the lake, Porter's Island to the west, and the town of Copper Harbor to the south.

Hunter's Point Park features two hiking trails, one north and another to the south. The trails are lush with trees and easy to travel. You can also take a 1.6-mile trail from the visitor center at Copper Harbor to the parking lot to see more sights from around the area.

Best Time to Visit: Conditions are tough during the winter season, so the summer is a better time for visiting the park.

Pass/Permit/Fees: You can enter the park for free.

Closest City or Town: Copper Harbor

How to Get There: You can take the walking trail from the Copper Harbor marina and visitor center to the park. You can also go north on North Coast Road from M-26 and then go right on Harbor Coast Lane. The town of Copper Harbor is accessible via US-41 from Marquette and L'Anse.

GPS Coordinates: 47.47466° N, 87.89833° W

Did You Know? Hunter's Point is the northernmost contiguous part of the state. The Isle Royale National Park is the only place further north in Michigan.

Isle Royale National Park

The Isle Royale National Park is the northernmost part of the state. The park is on an island that is only accessible by ferry. Isle Royale features about 160 miles of hiking trails. It is open for canoeing, kayaking, and fishing. You will find a few camping sites throughout the park, with some of these sites near wolf and moose habitats. You will also encounter many untapped rock formations and shores around the park. Native copper is the most common mineral you will find here.

Best Time to Visit: The park is accessible from May to September. Ferry services that support the park do not operate year round.

Pass/Permit/Fees: A round-trip ferry ride costs $150 per adult and $115 per child.

Closest City or Town: Copper Harbor

How to Get There: You can take a ferry from Copper Harbor to reach the island. The ferry will go to the Rock Harbor station on the northeastern end. There is also a ferry service to the west in Windigo, but that ferry station serves Minnesota. It takes about four hours for a ferry to go from Copper Harbor to Isle Royale.

GPS Coordinates: 48.07230° N, 88.62763° W

Did You Know? Isle Royale is the least-visited national park in the contiguous United States, with about 25,000 people visiting each year.

Arab American National Museum

The Arab American National Museum in Dearborn is the world's first museum dedicated to Arab history in the United States. The museum explores the lives of Arab Americans and their contributions to society.

This museum features exhibits on how Arabs came from the Middle East and North Africa to call the United States home. It explores their lives in America and how they make an impact on society today. The museum has stories about many famous Arab Americans who have made an impact like Helen Thomas, Jordyn Wieber, and Farouk El-Baz. There is also an art gallery that highlights various pieces of work from Arab Americans.

Best Time to Visit: The museum has a calendar of events showcasing different exhibits and programs for viewing listed on their website.

Pass/Permit/Fees: Admission to the museum is $8.

Closest City or Town: Dearborn

How to Get There: From Detroit, take I-94 west and then take Exit 210A to Michigan Avenue or US-12. Continue west, then turn right on Neckel Street and right again on the next road. The SmartBus 2 and 261 routes have a station nearby.

GPS Coordinates: 42.32226° N, 83.17657° W

Did You Know? Dearborn has one of the country's largest Arab-American populations. Nearly 40,000 people of Arab descent live here as of 2021.

The Henry Ford

The Henry Ford is a museum complex in Dearborn that celebrates American history. The museum houses many artifacts that belonged in Henry Ford's collection.

Some of the items you will find at the Henry Ford include a camp bed used by George Washington, a Dymaxion house from Buckminster Fuller, the chair at Ford's Theatre where Abraham Lincoln was shot, and the bus where Rosa Parks refused to surrender her seat.

You can also visit Greenfield Village while at the complex. The village features Henry Ford's birth home and a replica of Thomas Edison's Menlo Park laboratory.

Best Time to Visit: The museum is open year round, but some parts of the Greenfield Village may not be accessible during the winter.

Pass/Permit/Fees: Admission is $25 for adults and $19 for children.

Closest City or Town: Dearborn

How to Get There: From Detroit, take I-94 west, then take Exit 209 for Rotunda Drive. Turn right on Southfield Road and left on Village Road to reach the complex.

GPS Coordinates: 42.30552° N, 83.22465° W

Did You Know? The bicycle shop owned by the Wright Brothers was relocated from Ohio to Greenfield Village in 1937. Henry Ford oversaw the effort.

Two Hearted River

The Two Hearted River in Luce County in the Upper Peninsula runs for about 24 miles. It starts in the western part of Luce County and continues north, where it drains into Lake Superior.

The river snakes its way through the landscape before reaching the lake. It goes near the Two Hearted River State Forest, a site featuring multiple beach spaces. The lake offers camping sites along its body, and there are a few spaces where you can put in a small manually powered boat and sail down the water.

Best Time to Visit: The weather conditions are easier in the summer.

Pass/Permit/Fees: There is no charge to visit the river.

Closest City or Town: Deer Park

How to Get There: The river is on the far northern end of Luce County. Start your trip up there in Roberts Corner off of M-28. Go north on M-123, then go left on County Highway 407 at Fourmile Corner. Go right on County Highway 410 when you get near the lake, and you will start to see some of the camping spots around the river.

GPS Coordinates: 46.70774° N, 85.41375° W

Did You Know? The river is a popular site for recreational fishing and was reportedly an inspiration to Ernest Hemingway for some of his stories.

Ambassador Bridge

The Ambassador Bridge is a 7,500-foot bridge that goes between Detroit and Windsor. It is the continent's busiest border crossing, with at least 4,000 automobiles and 10,000 trucks going across it each day. The bridge opened in 1929 and features a suspension layout. The Ambassador Bridge starts near the Mexicantown neighborhood of Detroit and goes past the University of Windsor. There are duty-free shops on each side of the bridge. You can also see great views of downtown Detroit from the north on a clear day.

Best Time to Visit: The bridge is open 24 hours a day. Avoid visiting during traditional rush hours in the morning and late afternoon, as the bridge can be extremely busy then.

Pass/Permit/Fees: The toll heading into Canada is $5 USD, while the toll heading into the United States is $6.25 USD. You must have a valid passport or enhanced driver's license when crossing the bridge.

Closest City or Town: Detroit

How to Get There: Take I-96 east toward Detroit and then take Exit 192B to reach the northern end of the bridge. The southern end in Windsor is on northern Huron Church Road, or Highway 3.

GPS Coordinates: 42.31278° N, 83.07383° W

Did You Know? The Ambassador Bridge and the nearby underwater tunnel are the only two road crossings between the United States and Canada where you go south to enter Canada instead of north.

Belle Isle Park

Belle Isle Park is a small island in Detroit with nearly 1,000 acres of land. It is the most popular state park in Michigan, with nearly 4 million people visiting each year.

Belle Isle Park is home to the James Scott Memorial Fountain, a 1925 fountain with a central spray of about 125 feet. The Belle Isle Aquarium features more than 100 species of marine life on display. The Belle Isle Conservatory also houses many plants and trees in its indoor space.

The eastern end of the island offers a lighthouse, driving range, and a few fishing piers. The Detroit Yacht Club also has a marina to the north. The south houses the Belle Isle Casino, a 1908 building for public events.

Best Time to Visit: The summer season is the best time to visit when the waters around the area are more comfortable.

Pass/Permit/Fees: Admission prices for various attractions and rental costs for water equipment will vary.

Closest City or Town: Detroit

How to Get There: Go east on Jefferson Avenue from downtown Detroit, then turn right on Grand Avenue. You'll cross the MacArthur Bridge to reach the park.

GPS Coordinates: 42.33785° N, 82.98801° W

Did You Know? Belle Isle Park hosts the Detroit Grand Prix every year. The open-wheel auto race goes around the fountain and the west end of the park.

Charles H. Wright Museum of African American History

You will find the world's largest collection of African American historical artifacts at the Charles H. Wright Museum of African American History in Detroit. This museum on the campus of Wayne State University features 125,000 square feet of room. The museum offers exhibits on various ancient African kingdoms and the Middle Passage. It also includes a modern look at the Civil Rights movement. You will find documents from the Underground Railroad and letters from Rosa Parks and Malcom X along with an exhibit devoted to the Tuskegee Airmen.

Best Time to Visit: The museum hosts its annual African World Festival every August, and the Wright hosts special events every February in honor of Black History Month.

Pass/Permit/Fees: Admission is $15 for adults and $12 for seniors and children.

Closest City or Town: Detroit

How to Get There: The museum is on the eastern end of the Wayne State University campus. You can reach via East Warren Avenue in between I-75 and Woodward Avenue. The Warren Avenue station on the Q-Line light rail system is a few blocks to the west.

GPS Coordinates: 42.35920° N, 83.06091° W

Did You Know? Rosa Parks and Aretha Franklin both lay in state in the rotunda at the museum following their respective deaths in 2005 and 2018.

Comerica Park

Comerica Park is the home of the Detroit Tigers baseball club. The park opened in 2000 and remains one of the most popular in the sport. Comerica Park features a massive 15-foot tiger statue at the entrance and eight others in other locations, with two on top of the scoreboard. You'll also find a small carnival area with a carousel that features tigers instead of horses. The outfield area contains a large fountain that shoots water when the Tigers score a run. The outfield also has statues dedicated to famous Tigers figures, including Ty Cobb and broadcaster Ernie Harwell.

Best Time to Visit: Ballpark tours are available from June to September on Tuesdays and Fridays. You can also catch a fireworks show after games on Friday nights from June to August.

Pass/Permit/Fees: Tours are available for $6 per person.

Closest City or Town: Detroit

How to Get There: The stadium is on Adams Avenue and Brush Street near the I-75/375 interchange. It is also directly west of Ford Field, the home of the Detroit Lions. The Grand Circus Park station on the Q-Line and the Detroit People Mover is to the southwest.

GPS Coordinates: 42.33913° N, 83.04848° W

Did You Know? Comerica Park has also hosted outdoor hockey games for the Detroit Red Wings, multiple local college hockey teams, and the Windsor Spitfires junior team.

Detroit Historical Museum

The Detroit Historical Museum on the Wayne State University campus highlights the history of the city of Detroit. Many of the exhibits feature scenes from the city dating back to the eighteenth century. The museum's exhibits include Detroit's role in the Underground Railroad, the early shops that spread around Detroit in the nineteenth century, and how it became the country's automotive hub in the twentieth century. There are exhibits about local music and the many innovators and inventors who called Detroit home. The museum also has one of the country's largest model train displays.

Best Time to Visit: The museum has many changing exhibits, focusing on unique aspects of Detroit's history, which are found on the museum's website.

Pass/Permit/Fees: Admission is $10 for adults and $6 for children.

Closest City or Town: Detroit

How to Get There: Take Woodward Avenue north from downtown Detroit to reach the museum on Kirby Street to the left. The 4 Woodward bus route has a stop near the museum. The Ferry Street Q-Line station is to the north.

GPS Coordinates: 42.35986° N, 83.06718° W

Did You Know? The Meier Clock at the museum is one of the most elaborate in the world. The 1904 clock features multiple dials displaying the time in many places around the world, plus multiple figures that appear on the clock during specific times of the hour.

Detroit Institute of Arts Museum

The Detroit Institute of Arts on the Wayne State University Campus has more than 100 art galleries. You'll see an armor collection that once belonged to William Randolph Hearst when you enter the museum. The entrance also features many frescoes from Diego Rivera's *Detroit Industry* series. The collection offers many pieces of art from around the world. The museum also has smaller sections dedicated to French painters and the Old Masters from before 1800. A self-portrait of Vincent Van Gogh, and William-Adolphe Bouguereau's *Nut Gatherers*, are among the most popular paintings on display here. There is also a section of the museum dedicated to puppetry art.

Best Time to Visit: Visit the website to see what touring exhibits are coming. The museum has housed many exhibitions devoted to artists such as Picasso, Rembrandt, Charles Sheeler, Ansel Adams, and Annie Leibovitz.

Pass/Permit/Fees: Admission is $14 for adults and $6 for children.

Closest City or Town: Detroit

How to Get There: Take Woodward Avenue north from downtown Detroit, then turn right on Kirby Street. Go right on John R Street to reach the museum.

GPS Coordinates: 42.35950° N, 83.06455° W

Did You Know? Part of the original 1927 building where much of the museum is housed is designed to look like a European Gothic chapel.

Detroit–Windsor Tunnel

The Detroit–Windsor Tunnel is a unique engineering marvel that links the cities of Detroit and Windsor. The tunnel travels nearly 1 mile under the Detroit River as the two-lane road leads between the United States and Canada. The tunnel was built in 1930 with immersed steel tubes that were sunk into a trench in the bottom of the river. The design allows fresh air to come through the tunnel without causing water leaks. It also uses a ventilation system to ensure that vehicle exhaust can escape at each end of the tunnel. The tunnel is the second-busiest crossing between the United States and Canada, with about 12,000 vehicles going through each day.

Best Time to Visit: Visit on weekdays, as the duty-free shop in Windsor at the southern end of the tunnel is open on weekdays. The shop offers heavy discounts on fragrance, liquor, and jewelry products, among other items.

Pass/Permit/Fees: The toll is $5 USD or $6.25 CAD when heading to Windsor and $4.50 USD or $4.75 CAD when entering Detroit.

Closest City or Town: Detroit

How to Get There: The Detroit side of the tunnel is accessible on Randolph Street. The entrance to the Windsor side is on Goyeau Street and Wyandotte Street.

GPS Coordinates: 42.32789° N, 83.04151° W

Did You Know? You will require a passport or an enhanced driver's license to go between Detroit and Windsor.

Detroit Zoo

The Detroit Zoo features about 125 acres of zoological exhibits in Detroit's northwestern suburbs. The zoo contains more than 200 species of animals.

The Arctic Ring of Life has 4 acres of space for polar bears and gray seals. You'll also find a giraffe exhibit where you can feed a giraffe from a platform.

The river otter habitat features a glass wall on one side where visitors can get an eye-level view of these creatures. You can also see primates like lowland gorillas at the Great Apes of Harambee exhibit.

Best Time to Visit: Most of the events at the zoo occur in the spring and summer. The winter is also popular, and the fountain near the penguin house becomes an ice rink.

Pass/Permit/Fees: Admission to the zoo is $19 for adults and $15 for children.

Closest City or Town: Detroit

How to Get There: The zoo is about 14 miles northwest of downtown Detroit in the towns of Huntington Woods and Royal Oak. Take I-75 north from downtown Detroit, and take Exit 61 to I-696 West. Take Exit 16 on I-696 to West 10 Mile Road. You'll find the zoo to the right.

GPS Coordinates: 42.47688° N, 83.14906° W

Did You Know? The Polk Penguin Conservation Center at the zoo is the world's largest penguin habitat.

Ford Piquette Avenue Plant

The Ford Piquette Avenue Plant was one of the Ford Motor Company's first automotive assembly plants. It was built in 1904 and was the first site where the iconic Model T vehicle was produced. You can visit the plant and see where the Model T and many other famous Ford vehicles were made. The refurbished plant features a re-creation of Henry Ford's office. You will also see many of the rooms where Ford vehicles were assembled. The plant highlights the assembly line approach used in production. You can also see reproductions of some of the vehicles that were produced at the plant, from the 1904 Model B to the 1909 Model T. There are also a few 1910s and 1920s vehicles from Studebaker on display. Studebaker acquired the building in the 1910s.

Best Time to Visit: The plant hosts a car show every September around the anniversary of the production of the first Model T.

Pass/Permit/Fees: Admission is $12 per person.

Closest City or Town: Detroit

How to Get There: The plant is in Detroit's Medbury Park neighborhood. Take Exit 215C from I-94 to Edsel Ford Service Drive, then go north on Beaubien Boulevard. The 42 bus route has a station to the south.

GPS Coordinates: 42.36867° N, 83.06525° W

Did You Know? The fire sprinkler system inside the building was a rare feature at the time.

Fox Theatre

The Fox Theatre is an old movie palace in downtown Detroit that now houses concerts and theater performances. The venue opened in 1928 as one of the theaters in the Fox Theatres chain run by William Fox.

The building features many Persian, Chinese, and Indian motifs on the inside. The venue includes three separate seating levels with a capacity of 5,000 people.

The outside holds a distinct marquee that covers much of the front. You'll notice the two Fox griffins on the sides.

Best Time to Visit: Tours are available throughout the year, although the timing for them will vary based on the schedule of events.

Pass/Permit/Fees: The prices for tours and events will vary throughout the year.

Closest City or Town: Detroit

How to Get There: The theater is on Woodward Avenue in the middle of downtown Detroit. It is one block west of Comerica Park. The Montcalm Street Q-Line rail station is to the northeast.

GPS Coordinates: 42.33858° N, 83.05240° W

Did You Know? The Fox Theatre is in part of the building that houses the headquarters to the Little Caesars pizza company and Olympia Entertainment, a group that owns the Detroit Tigers and Red Wings sports teams.

GM Renaissance Center

The GM Renaissance Center in Detroit is the tallest building in the state. The building is 727 feet high and features a 73-story hotel tower surrounded by four 39-story office towers. The center offers a vast dining and shopping space on the bottom level. The bottom also houses a 5-story glass atrium for public events. You can see various General Motors vehicles on display at the *GM World* exhibit while at the center. The top part of the hotel tower features an observation deck. You can see Detroit and other surroundings from nearly 30 miles out.

Best Time to Visit: The summer is a good time to visit since there are more public events during that season.

Pass/Permit/Fees: You can visit the center for free, but it costs extra to visit some of the attractions. The observation deck is not always open, as special events in the area might keep it closed. Check with the center to see if the deck is open first before arriving.

Closest City or Town: Detroit

How to Get There: Take the Beaubien Boulevard exit south from Jefferson Avenue to reach the center. The Detroit–Windsor Tunnel is also to the east of the tower and provides a direct link to Jefferson Avenue. The building has a Detroit People Mover light rail station.

GPS Coordinates: 42.32943° N, 83.03978° W

Did You Know? The tower became the tallest in Detroit in 1977, surpassing the Penobscot Building by about 160 feet.

Historic Fort Wayne

You will find Historic Fort Wayne in the Delray neighborhood of southern Detroit. The fort complex features a limestone barracks building constructed in 1848 and a fort from around the same time with a brick exterior.

There are multiple buildings overlooking the Detroit River. You'll see a few gun emplacements and officers' houses throughout the area. There is also a powder magazine near the barracks with a distinct limestone design. Many of the sites around here were active during the Civil War, as there were concerns about a possible attack from Canada.

Best Time to Visit: The fort is open from May to October every year. It is open on weekends, although group visits are available by appointment on weekdays.

Pass/Permit/Fees: Admission is $5 per person.

Closest City or Town: Detroit

How to Get There: The fort is about 2 miles south of Ambassador Bridge. Take M-85 or Fort Street south from downtown Detroit, then go south on Livernois Avenue to reach the fort.

GPS Coordinates: 42.29993° N, 83.09583° W

Did You Know? The fort is the third to have been built in Detroit, but it was also the first one to have been built by Americans.

Little Caesars Arena

The Little Caesars Arena in Detroit is the home of the Detroit Red Wings hockey team and the Detroit Pistons basketball team. The arena opened in 2017 and is one of the country's most inviting sports venues.

This arena features a glass roof built to create a street-like atmosphere around the concourses. The venue also hosts multiple restaurants for pre-event dining. The arena houses many statues of Detroit sports legends like Gordie Howe and Ted Lindsay. Chevrolet also has an art installation that features the Red Wings logo made out of many Chevrolet automobile parts.

Best Time to Visit: The arena is open for tours throughout the year. You'll have an easier time getting a tour in the summer.

Pass/Permit/Fees: Prices for entry and tours will vary throughout the year.

Closest City or Town: Detroit

How to Get There: The arena is on Woodward Avenue in Detroit, directly north of the Fisher Freeway, or I-75. The Sproat Street station on the Q-Line light rail train has a station here.

GPS Coordinates: 42.34117° N, 83.05526° W

Did You Know? The original outdoor sign letters from the Detroit Olympia are on display inside the arena concourse. The Detroit Olympia housed the Red Wings from 1927 to 1979.

Masonic Temple of Detroit

Detroit's Masonic Temple is the largest Masonic temple in the world. The temple has more than 1,000 rooms that can be used for concerts, photo shoots, weddings, seminars, and conferences. The most prominent part of the temple is the Masonic Theater, a performance hall with room for about 4,600 people. The theater is inside a stunning Gothic Revival–inspired building. The venue also houses the smaller Jack White Theater and the elaborate Crystal Ballroom. Many of the decorations around the temple include motifs from the Gothic, Romanesque, and Egyptian styles. Parts of these motifs surround the old Commandery Asylum for the Knights Templar.

Best Time to Visit: The temple hosts tours on the first and third Sundays of each month.

Pass/Permit/Fees: Tours are $25 per person. You can also schedule a tour at a different time outside of Sunday, but it costs $40 per person.

Closest City or Town: Detroit

How to Get There: The temple is across from Cass Park on Temple Street and Cass Avenue. You can reach Temple Street by going west off of Woodward Avenue. There is also an exit to the road on M-10 South. DDOT bus route 23 has a station nearby.

GPS Coordinates: 42.34175° N, 83.06016° W

Did You Know? The stage at the Masonic Theater is one of the world's largest, as it is about 100 feet wide between the walls.

Motown Museum

You will find the Motown Museum in the Hitsville USA building on West Grand Boulevard in Detroit. The house was utilized for much of the 1960s as the headquarters of the iconic Motown music label.

The Motown Museum features many artifacts from some of the artists and groups that recorded for Motown. You can visit a re-creation of one of the recording studios here. You'll also find many instruments and promotional materials from some of Motown's most famous artists. There is also an 1877 Steinway grand piano on display that the label inherited.

Best Time to Visit: The museum is open throughout the year.

Pass/Permit/Fees: Admission is $15 for adults and $10 for seniors and children.

Closest City or Town: Detroit

How to Get There: Take M-10 northwest from downtown Detroit, then take Exit 4C to Milwaukee Avenue. Go left on Milwaukee Avenue, then go left on Lincoln Street and right on Holden Street. Go left on Grand Avenue, and you'll find the museum on the right. Bus route 16 also has a nearby station.

GPS Coordinates: 42.36424° N, 83.08850° W

Did You Know? The most noteworthy artifact at the museum is a black fedora hat and a sequined glove from Michael Jackson.

Pewabic Pottery

The Pewabic Pottery school in Detroit has been producing glazes for many buildings throughout Michigan and other parts of the country since 1903. The current 1908 building that houses the school is open for tours. You can even take a pottery class at the school if you're interested.

The Pewabic Pottery building houses various pieces of pottery work from the past 100 years. You'll learn about how pottery devices are produced and how glazes for buildings are prepared. These include some of the iridescent coatings that you'll find around many Detroit properties.

Best Time to Visit: The pottery school starts its classes in the fall season.

Pass/Permit/Fees: Pottery workshops can cost from $50 to $100 depending on the activity and time of the year. Many weekend-long workshops are open, while some eight-week programs are also available.

Closest City or Town: Detroit

How to Get There: The pottery house is on East Jefferson Avenue. Take the road about 4 miles from downtown Detroit to reach the house.

GPS Coordinates: 42.36212° N, 82.98169° W

Did You Know? Some of the buildings that feature glazes produced by the Pewabic Pottery house include the Basilica of the National Shrine of the Immaculate Conception in Washington and the Shedd Aquarium in Chicago.

The Spirit of Detroit

The *Spirit of Detroit* is an iconic statue in the heart of downtown Detroit. The statue is at the Coleman A. Young Municipal Center.

The 1958 bronze sculpture by Marshall Fredericks features a seated man holding a sphere symbolizing God in his left hand and a family group in his right hand. The statue symbolizes that one's faith is expressed in one's family and that the relationship with one's family is the strongest one can hold.

Best Time to Visit: You can see the statue throughout the year, but sometimes the statue is decorated with different features based on specific events. For example, it often wears the jersey of local sports teams.

Pass/Permit/Fees: The statue is free to visit.

Closest City or Town: Detroit

How to Get There: The *Spirit of Detroit* is at the southern end of Woodward Avenue by Jefferson Avenue. The Congress Street Q-Line is near the statue, as are the 3, 5, 6, 9, 40, 52, and 67 bus routes.

GPS Coordinates: 42.32927° N, 83.04453° W

Did You Know? You'll find another iconic sculpture a block south at the *Monument to Joe Louis*. The sculpture is a hanging bronze image of a fist to celebrate the famous boxer.

Tiger Stadium Site

The former site of Tiger Stadium in Detroit is a popular site for baseball fans to visit while in the city. The site on the corner of Michigan Avenue and Trumbull Avenue was home to the Detroit Tigers baseball club from 1912 to 1999.

Tiger Stadium is where many Tigers icons like Ty Cobb and Al Kaline played. It also hosted three MLB All-Star Games. This is where Lou Gehrig benched himself before a game in 1939, ending his then-record streak of consecutive games played. The site is currently home to the Corner Ballpark, a venue that hosts various local high school baseball games.

Best Time to Visit: The place is open to visit throughout the baseball season.

Pass/Permit/Fees: You can visit the site for free.

Closest City or Town: Detroit

How to Get There: Tiger Stadium site is about 1.5 miles west of downtown Detroit. Take US-12 or Michigan Avenue west from the center, and you'll find the site on the corner of Trumbull Avenue. DDOT bus routes 2 and 261 have a stop there as well.

GPS Coordinates: 42.33217° N, 83.06870° W

Did You Know? The site features a small exhibit at the Corner Ballpark office with multiple artifacts from Tiger Stadium on display. This includes a few wooden seats dating back to the early twentieth century.

Hudson Mills Metropark

The Hudson Mills Metropark in Dexter is along part of the Huron River in Washtenaw County. The park features a segment of the Border-to-Border Trail that makes its way toward Ann Arbor and Ypsilanti.

Hudson Mills features about 1,500 acres of land. There is an 18-hole golf course at the park, along with a few disc golf courses, a playground for the kids, and some softball diamonds. You can also rent a canoe from the local area and go paddling down part of the Huron River.

Best Time to Visit: The summer is ideal when the golf course has more openings and the trails around the park are easier to traverse.

Pass/Permit/Fees: The park is free to enter, but it will cost extra for you to schedule a time at the golf course or reserve a canoe rental.

Closest City or Town: Dexter

How to Get There: The park is around the northern end of the town of Dexter. You can reach Dexter by taking Baker Road north from I-94.

GPS Coordinates: 42.36083° N, 83.90552° W

Did You Know? The longest hiking trail at the park goes from a small subdivision to the south near Dexter to the northern end of the park. You'll come across a few of the holes on the golf course as you walk down the trail.

Abrams Planetarium

The Abrams Planetarium is located on the campus of Michigan State University in East Lansing. It is operated by the university's Department of Physics and Astronomy. The planetarium offers an exhibit hall highlighting various astronomical discoveries. Part of the hall features a black-light gallery where you'll see fluorescent images lit by ultraviolet lights. The sky theater contains a 50-foot dome that works as a projection screen.

Best Time to Visit: The venue hosts public shows on Saturdays and Sundays. Outdoor observations are held on Saturdays when the sky conditions are right.

Pass/Permit/Fees: Tickets are $5.50 for adults and $4.50 for children.

Closest City or Town: East Lansing

How to Get There: The planetarium is south of the Red Cedar River on MSU campus. Take Bogue Street south off of Grand River Road or M-43, then turn right on Shaw Lane. The planetarium is across the street from Shaw Hall. CATA bus routes 20, 22, and 23 also have stops near the venue.

GPS Coordinates: 42.72562° N, 84.47628° W

Did You Know? The planetarium offers a monthly newsletter called *Sky Calendar* where you can review the positions of the moon, planets, and various constellations throughout the month.

Beaumont Tower

Beaumont Tower is the most iconic structure on Michigan State University's campus in East Lansing. The tower was built in 1928 and stands about 104 feet high.

Beaumont Tower is a Collegiate Gothic tower with an Art Deco bas-relief on its front area. It features a carillon with 49 bells that chime on the hour throughout the day.

You'll notice one of the finials on top is higher than the others. The shorter three finials represent the importance of higher education.

Best Time to Visit: Visit during the summer season when the campus isn't as crowded.

Pass/Permit/Fees: While you can go outside the tower for free, entrance to the inside is off-limits to non-campus personnel.

Closest City or Town: East Lansing

How to Get There: The tower is inside Circle Drive on MSU campus between the Music Practice Building and Linton Hall. Take the East Michigan Avenue exit off of M-43, then go west. Turn left on Beal Street, then keep straight on Circle Drive. The tower is near the southeastern part of the circle.

GPS Coordinates: 42.73200° N, 84.48219° W

Did You Know? The tower is on the site where College Hall once stood, which was the first building to be constructed on MSU campus.

MSU Museum

The MSU Museum is on the Michigan State University campus in East Lansing. The Smithsonian-affiliated museum hosts many collections on nature and human cultures from around Michigan. You will find thousands of artifacts from nineteenth and twentieth-century life around the Great Lakes region. There is also an anthropology collection housing many items producing by indigenous peoples who once lived in the area.

The museum also has a folklore section that tells the stories of many of the area's people, highlighting the unique expressions of identity of those who once called the state home.

Best Time to Visit: Visit the museum's website to see what traveling exhibitions are coming to the museum.

Pass/Permit/Fees: The museum is free to visit, although a $5 donation is recommended.

Closest City or Town: East Lansing

How to Get There: The museum is on Circle Drive on the MSU campus. Take East Michigan Avenue east toward campus, then turn right on Beal Street. Go left on Circle Drive, and continue one way toward the southeastern end of the road.

GPS Coordinates: 42.73160° N, 84.48170° W

Did You Know? The museum houses various fossils found throughout the state.

Torch Lake

Torch Lake is a narrow lake on the northern part of the Lower Peninsula. At nearly 20 miles long, you'll find many things to experience around the lake.

Torch Lake features spots for boating, with ramps on both the northern and southern ends. There are a few spots for swimming around the lake, with many of these sites offering clean and clear water.

Best Time to Visit: The Torch Lake Fireworks Show is the most popular event at the lake. The show occurs every year on July 3 and starts at the southern end.

Pass/Permit/Fees: You can reach the lake for free, but it may cost extra to use one of the boating docks.

Closest City or Town: Eastport

How to Get There: Torch Lake is east of US-31, which goes from Traverse City to the south and Charlevoix to the north.

GPS Coordinates: 45.07716° N, 85.35800° W

Did You Know? There are multiple vacation homes on the shore of the lake. Some of these homes offer private beach access. You can rent many of these throughout the year, although the availability may be limited.

Eben Ice Caves

The Eben Ice Caves are in the northwestern part of the Hiawatha National Forest in the Upper Peninsula, south of Silver Creek.

The Eben Ice Caves are formed by melting snow running over a cliff and freezing. You will find formations of varying sizes and lengths hanging from around the caves, producing one of the most beautiful scenes in the state. The water from the nearby Silver Creek helps produce these ice buildups.

Best Time to Visit: You likely won't see much freezing water during the summer, so visit during the winter.

Pass/Permit/Fees: The local landowners allow people to reach the ice caves for free.

Closest City or Town: Eben Junction

How to Get There: The caves are about 1 mile northeast of the Eben Ice Caves trailhead near Eben Junction. Eben Junction is accessible off of US-41 to the west. Go east on M-94 through Rumley, then turn left on Eben Road when you reach Eben Junction. Turn right on Frey Road to reach the trailhead.

GPS Coordinates: 46.38330° N, 86.94402° W

Did You Know? The hike is short, but ice cleats are strongly recommended for helping you keep your grip when hiking to the caves.

Empire Bluff Trail

The Sleeping Bear Dunes National Lakeshore is on the northwestern part of the Upper Peninsula. The most popular part of the shoreline is to the south near the town of Empire. The Empire Bluff Trail is a 0.75-mile trail that goes from Wilco Road to the east to the Empire Bluffs to the west, revealing a dynamic view of Lake Michigan.

The hilly trail leads you through many dune plants and maple trees. You'll find a view of Lake Michigan from up high on a boardwalk at the end.

Best Time to Visit: Visit any time outside of the winter, as the boardwalk and bluffs are closed off during this season. Ice and snow conditions during the winter make those areas dangerous.

Pass/Permit/Fees: The trail is free to visit.

Closest City or Town: Empire

How to Get There: The eastern end of the trail is on Wilco Road, which is south of Empire from South Lake Street. The town of Empire is about 25 miles west of Traverse City. Take M-72 West all the way from Traverse City to reach Empire.

GPS Coordinates: 44.80150° N, 86.06644° W

Did You Know? There are a few pieces of old farm equipment in the middle of the trail, marking where an old farm was once found in the area.

Grand Haven City Beach

The Grand Haven City Beach is in the southeastern part of Grand Haven. The beach is popular for swimming, as it includes many open spots that lead into Lake Michigan. You'll also find sandy places to relax while there.

The beach is popular with dog owners, as dogs are allowed on a leash in the morning and evening hours during the season. The area provides a relaxing spot for dog walking.

Best Time to Visit: The water is the most comfortable during the summer season. Dog owners should arrive after Labor Day or before Memorial Day, as dogs are allowed on-leash during all hours instead of only in the morning and evening.

Pass/Permit/Fees: The beach does not charge admission. Free parking is available, but the spots are limited.

Closest City or Town: Grand Haven

How to Get There: The beach is on South Harbor Drive in Grand Haven. You can take Jackson Street west from US-31 in the middle of town to reach the beach. Jackson Street soon becomes Harbor Drive, which continues down south along the Grand River and eventually to Lake Michigan.

GPS Coordinates: 43.05188° N, 86.24487° W

Did You Know? The beach hosts various weddings throughout the year, but all weddings must take place south of the restaurant.

Blandford Nature Center

The Blandford Nature Center in northwestern Grand Rapids is a park area featuring various animal habitats. The center houses 13 different trails that go around multiple nature sites. You'll see many trees, including maple and birch. The center is a prominent site for birdwatching, as you can find owls and many other birds of prey at the aviary here. There is also a reptile house that features a turtle den. The center has a farm area where kids can learn about various animals. There is also a playground in the farm space itself.

Best Time to Visit: The center is open Monday through Saturday. You'll find some of the most popular events here during the summer.

Pass/Permit/Fees: The center is free to visit, but a donation of at least $6 per person is recommended.

Closest City or Town: Grand Rapids

How to Get There: The center is about 6 miles northwest of downtown Grand Rapids. Take MI-45 from the middle of the city and go west, turning right on Collindale Avenue. Go left on Leonard Street and then right on Hillburn Avenue.

GPS Coordinates: 42.99576° N, 85.73943° W

Did You Know? The center offers a lesson on animal tracks. You can learn to identify animals based on their prints.

Brewery Vivant

The Brewery Vivant is located in one of the most intriguing venues in the Grand Rapids area. The brewery is inside a former chapel and funeral home. It operates with a green approach, using sustainable items found throughout Michigan and prioritizing organic farming efforts to produce the ingredients for its beers.

The Brewery Vivant serves many types of beer, including a few German-inspired beers and draft cocktails. It also offers separate lunch and dinner menus, with many of the meals featuring French-inspired accents.

Best Time to Visit: Any time is good to visit, as the brewery takes reservations for dining inside the property. You could also go to the patio for no-reservations dining, although it may be tough to find a spot there.

Pass/Permit/Fees: The prices will vary based on what you order, but you can expect to get a meal and a drink for about $20 on average.

Closest City or Town: Grand Rapids

How to Get There: The brewery is in the East Hills neighborhood in the eastern part of Grand Rapids. Take Fulton Street east from downtown to Lake Drive, then go right on Abney Avenue and left on Cherry Street to reach the brewery.

GPS Coordinates: 42.95979° N, 85.64614° W

Did You Know? The brewery houses private events throughout the year.

Calvin Ecosystem Preserve & Native Gardens

The Calvin Ecosystem Preserve & Native Gardens in Grand Rapids feature 100 acres of native plants and multiple spots for birdwatching. The area hosts nearly 170 species of native plants. Plus, close to 200 birds have been spotted in the preserve. There is also a main trail that goes through most of the wooded area.

The preserve is part of Calvin University, a Christian school in Grand Rapids. The school also maintains two ponds on the northern and southern ends of the preserve.

Best Time to Visit: The summer is the best time to visit, as the park hosts various volunteer days. People can help plant and harvest many of the native plants found throughout the area.

Pass/Permit/Fees: You can visit the preserve for free, but it costs extra to participate in educational programs.

Closest City or Town: Grand Rapids

How to Get There: The preserve is in the northeastern part of the Calvin University campus. Take Exit 38 on I-196 to Beltline Avenue, then continue south on the road until you reach the campus area.

GPS Coordinates: 42.93203° N, 85.58224° W

Did You Know? College programs inside the preserve study various animals and plants that are found in the area.

Frederik Meijer Gardens & Sculpture Park

The Frederik Meijer Gardens & Sculpture Park is a park space in Grand Rapids featuring more than 150 acres of land. The area offers a conservatory with nearly 15,000 square feet of room for tropical plants. You will find banana and bamboo trees throughout the indoor environment. You'll also find a Japanese garden with bonsai trees and many Zen-style arrangements. Other features include a woodland plant garden and a nature trail that leads to local wetlands. The sculpture park holds multiple sculptures from different parts of the world. One of the sculptures is a 24-foot horse designed in homage to a similar sculpture by Da Vinci.

Best Time to Visit: The park hosts the *Butterflies Are Blooming* exhibit in March and April, which features thousands of butterflies from around the world.

Pass/Permit/Fees: Admission for adults is $14.50 and $7 for children.

Closest City or Town: Grand Rapids

How to Get There: Take I-196 East from downtown Grand Rapids. Take Exit 38 to M-44 North, then go right to reach the garden.

GPS Coordinates: 42.97971° N, 85.58569° W

Did You Know? The park takes its name from Frederik Meijer, the founder of the Meijer superstore chain. Meijer donated the land for the park in 1991.

Fulton Street Farmers Market

The Fulton Street Farmers Market is one of the oldest markets of its kind in Michigan. It has been operating in Grand Rapids since 1922.

The market features more than 100 outdoor and indoor booths where you can find various local products. These include produce, arts and crafts items, and dairy goods. You can also find some wines and beer from local groups and even body care products. All items are made in Michigan and are available for sale throughout the year.

Best Time to Visit: You'll find an art market here during the summer months.

Pass/Permit/Fees: Each vendor at the market will charge their own rates for different items available for sale.

Closest City or Town: Grand Rapids

How to Get There: Fulton Street is in the eastern part of Grand Rapids. You can reach the area from I-196 by going south on the Fuller Avenue exit. You'll find the market to the right from that road.

GPS Coordinates: 42.96377° N, 85.64036° W

Did You Know? The vendors at the market have been a part of local festivities for generations, including some that have been present since the 1930s.

Gerald R. Ford Presidential Museum

The Gerald R. Ford Presidential Museum in Grand Rapids illustrates Ford's life and his work as a representative for Michigan. It also includes exhibits on Ford's term as the 38th President of the United States. The museum features thousands of artifacts surrounding Ford's work. There is a replica of his Oval Office and a look at the 1976 Bicentennial celebration held by Ford. There are also various artifacts about First Lady Elizabeth Anne Ford and a cabinet room exhibit. The museum also has an exhibit surrounding the Watergate crisis that led to Ford becoming president after Richard Nixon and Spiro Agnew's resignations. You'll also see a piece of the Berlin Wall in the lobby. Gerald and Elizabeth Ford's final resting places are on the museum grounds.

Best Time to Visit: The museum hosts various events around Ford's birthday on July 14.

Pass/Permit/Fees: Admission is $10 for adults, $8 for seniors, and $4 for children.

Closest City or Town: Grand Rapids

How to Get There: The museum is between Michigan and Pearl streets in northwestern Grand Rapids. You can reach these streets off of US-131 to the west.

GPS Coordinates: 42.96864° N, 85.67752° W

Did You Know? The Gerald R. Ford Presidential Library is in Ann Arbor. Ford's museum is the only presidential museum to be separate from that person's presidential library.

Golf Club at Thornapple Pointe

You will enjoy some of the best views of the Thornapple River in Grand Rapids at the Golf Club at Thornapple Pointe. The club features an 18-hole course that goes along many beautiful rolling hills. You will see various forested areas around some of the holes on the golf course. Some of the holes go along a bend in the river. The course hosts many tournaments and private events throughout the year. It also offers instruction to new golfers looking to build their skills.

Best Time to Visit: The summer makes it easier to find an open tee time, especially since you won't be subject to frost delays.

Pass/Permit/Fees: The cost for golfing here will vary throughout the year. You will need reservations to golf at any time.

Closest City or Town: Grand Rapids

How to Get There: The course is west of the Thornapple River and east of the Gerald Ford Airport. Take I-96 East from downtown Grand Rapids, then take Exit 44 to 36th Street. Continue east on the road, which soon becomes Thornapple River Drive. Turn left on 48th Street to reach the course.

GPS Coordinates: 42.87812° N, 85.48791° W

Did You Know? The course offers a golf simulator where you can play on a virtual version of real golf courses from around the world. The LiveGolf simulator offers virtual versions of the Pebble Beach and St. Andrews courses.

68

Grand Rapids Art Museum

The Grand Rapids Art Museum houses more than 5,000 pieces of art, showcasing the world of art from the Renaissance period through the twentieth century.

The museum houses noteworthy paintings from famous artists like Richard Diebenkorn, Albrecht Dürer, Jacob Lawrence, and Winslow Homer. There is also a print room and reference library you can visit by appointment that houses many prints dating back to the eighteenth century.

Best Time to Visit: Admission is free on Tuesdays as part of a partnership with the Grand Rapids–based Meijer superstore chain. Don't forget to also visit their website to see what touring exhibits are at the museum before you visit.

Pass/Permit/Fees: Admission is $10 for adults and $6 for children. Some touring exhibits may require a separate ticket for admission.

Closest City or Town: Grand Rapids

How to Get There: The museum is in downtown Grand Rapids next to Rosa Parks Circle. Take US-131 to Cherry Street, then go east on the road. Turn left on Ionia Avenue, then go left on Louis Street to reach the museum. The Rapid bus routes 6, 13, 45, and 90 all have stops near the venue.

GPS Coordinates: 42.96502° N, 85.67105° W

Did You Know? The 2004 building that houses the museum is the world's first LEED-certified art museum.

Grand Rapids Children's Museum

The Grand Rapids Children's Museum houses many exhibits for kids to see on two floors. The museum's most famous attraction is the Live Hive, a spot featuring a live beehive. Other exhibits include Kristen's Corner, a place where children can learn how instruments make various sounds.

Other features at the museum include an exhibit on how emergency service workers operate and another spot on how centrifugal force works. The museum also has an old Volkswagen Beetle vehicle on display.

Best Time to Visit: The museum hosts an annual Day of Play Celebration every July. The festival sponsors activities throughout different parks in downtown Grand Rapids.

Pass/Permit/Fees: Tickets are $9.

Closest City or Town: Grand Rapids

How to Get There: The museum is west of Veterans Memorial Park in downtown Grand Rapids. Take the Ottawa Avenue exit on I-196 south to Monroe Center Street, then continue east until you reach the park area.

GPS Coordinates: 42.96398° N, 85.66716° W

Did You Know? The museum offers many spots that are wheelchair accessible.

Grand Rapids Public Museum

The Grand Rapids Public Museum is inside an old flour mill on the western shore of the Grand River. The museum houses exhibits on the history of Grand Rapids, Native American life in the area, and the wildlife of the Grand River.

The museum features a 1928 Spillman carousel. There is also a virtual reality room where you can see various unique scenes from Grand Rapids history and interact with many digital surroundings. You'll also see art exhibits at the museum dedicated to different cultures and trends throughout Grand Rapids.

Best Time to Visit: The museum features many touring and temporary exhibits. Visit the website for the latest information on what you will find there.

Pass/Permit/Fees: Admission is $13 for adults and $8 for children.

Closest City or Town: Grand Rapids

How to Get There: The museum is south of the Pearl Street Bridge in downtown Grand Rapids. You can exit on Pearl Street from US-131 and go east on the road, turning right on Front Avenue. The Rapid bus routes 9 and 20 serve the northern end of the museum campus.

GPS Coordinates: 42.96560° N, 85.67673° W

Did You Know? The museum houses a 1928 Wurlitzer pipe organ and hosts music performances on the organ throughout the year.

John Ball Zoo

The John Ball Zoo in John Ball Park in Grand Rapids houses more than 200 species of animals. The zoo features a series of habitats for animals throughout the world. You will find such mammals as the African lion, the grizzly bear, and the tiger. There are many birds of prey on display as well, including the bald eagle and the great horned owl.

The reptile file at the zoo has Komodo dragons and American alligators. The zoo has one of the largest alligator habitats outside of Florida. You can also see leopard and nurse sharks and cownose rays at the aquarium at the zoo.

Best Time to Visit: The zoo is open from March to November every year. It is not open from December to February, as many of the animals will be hibernating and will need to be kept safe from inclement weather conditions during the winter months.

Pass/Permit/Fees: Admission is $12 for adults and $10 for children.

Closest City or Town: Grand Rapids

How to Get There: The zoo is on the eastern end of the Gerald Ford Freeway, or I-196. Take the Fulton Street West exit from the freeway east. You'll find an entrance to the zoo on the right.

GPS Coordinates: 42.96242° N, 85.70361° W

Did You Know? The Bissell Tree House on the northern part of the zoo is a popular site for private events.

Meyer May House

The Meyer May House in Grand Rapids was designed by Frank Lloyd Wright and dates back to 1909. The house highlights the Prairie School design that Wright used in many of his buildings. You'll notice the long horizontal lines around the outside of the house alongside prominent overhanging eaves. The house features multiple windows with symmetrical patterns. The first-floor windows are raised to provide light to the second floor and offer privacy. The dividing wall between the living and dining rooms features a mural with hollyhocks.

Best Time to Visit: The house is open for tours on Tuesdays, Thursdays, and Sundays.

Pass/Permit/Fees: Admission to the house is free. The Grand Rapids–based Steelcase office furniture company owns the property and was responsible for a massive restoration project. The company keeps the property open to everyone.

Closest City or Town: Grand Rapids

How to Get There: The house is on Madison Avenue southeast of downtown Grand Rapids. Go east of Fulton Street from downtown Grand Rapids, then turn right on College Avenue. Go right on Logan Street, and you will find the house to the right.

GPS Coordinates: 42.95434° N, 85.65888° W

Did You Know? The house has been restored to its original 1909 condition, with many of the original pieces of furniture and other furnishings intact.

Urban Institute for Contemporary Arts

The Urban Institute for Contemporary Arts in Grand Rapids is a facility operated by Ferris State University. The institute hosts many exhibits and programs on contemporary art, including visual arts, dance, film, and music.

The museum holds conferences throughout the year that focus on understanding the unique world of art and how it has evolved. The venue challenges participants to see the world in a new light.

Best Time to Visit: You can find many traveling exhibits at the institute throughout the year, which are listed on the institute's website.

Pass/Permit/Fees: The UICA does not charge admission.

Closest City or Town: Grand Rapids

How to Get There: The UICA is on Pearl Street in the northern part of downtown Grand Rapids. You can reach the area off of I-196 via the Ottawa Avenue exit.

GPS Coordinates: 42.96675° N, 85.66866° W

Did You Know? Many of the public art pieces at the UICA are made by various local artists from around Grand Rapids.

Tunnel of Trees

The Tunnel of Trees on M-119 in the northern Lower Peninsula runs for about 20 miles. The narrow road goes along the Little Traverse Bay and brings you through various scenic sites. You'll find many country stores, restaurants, and pit stops all around the area.

The Tunnel of Trees features various evergreen and hardwood trees surrounding the road. The trees stretch outward over the road to create a tunnel-like effect.

Best Time to Visit: The yellow and orange colors of the trees during the fall season are among the most beautiful sights you will find in the state.

Pass/Permit/Fees: You can drive the route for free.

Closest City or Town: Harbor Springs

How to Get There: The best way to reach the Tunnel of Trees is to start at the southern end in Harbor Springs. Take US-31 to Conway, then go west on Conway Road. Merge right on M-119, and continue into the town of Harbor Springs. The route continues north until Cross Village.

GPS Coordinates: 45.42989° N, 84.99296° W

Did You Know? The town of Good Hart is the midway point of the Tunnel of Trees. You'll find a church in the area near a Jesuit mission dating to the eighteenth century.

Silver Lake Sand Dunes

The Silver Lake Sand Dunes of Oceana County feature about 3,000 acres of land and 4 miles of shoreline on Lake Michigan. The sand dunes are the only ones east of the Mississippi River that people can traverse in an off-road vehicle.

You'll find many small dune buggies driving along the sand dunes throughout the season.

Best Time to Visit: It is easier to go through the sand dunes in the summer.

Pass/Permit/Fees: You can visit the sand dunes for free, but it will cost money to rent a dune buggy or other off-road vehicle. The cost for a rental will vary.

Closest City or Town: Hart

How to Get There: Take the Polk Road exit off of US-31 and travel west. Go right on 56th Avenue, then take a left on Deer Road. Go right on Juniper Beach Road, then take a left on Ridge Road to reach the sand dunes.

GPS Coordinates: 43.67619° N, 86.51286° W

Did You Know? You will find the Little Sable Point Lighthouse to the south of the dunes.

Saugatuck Dunes State Park

The Saugatuck Dunes State Park in Allegan County features about 2.5 miles of shoreline along Lake Michigan. The coastal dunes at the park are more than 200 feet tall. Many of these dunes lead people directly to the shoreline.

The park is north of the Oxbow Lagoon and Tallmadge Woods Nature Preserve. You will find a small opening on the Kalamazoo River toward Lake Michigan in the area. You can reach that opening on a boat from the state park.

Best Time to Visit: The area is the most accessible during the summer season.

Pass/Permit/Fees: You can reach the park for free.

Closest City or Town: Holland

How to Get There: Take the Blue Star Highway exit off of I-196, and go west on the road. Take a right on 64th Street, then go west on 140th Avenue to reach the park.

GPS Coordinates: 42.70428° N, 86.20095° W

Did You Know? The park is a popular place for birdwatching.

Windmill Island

Windmill Island in Holland is a 36-acre park that houses the De Zwaan windmill. The windmill dates to the mid-eighteenth century and is the only fully functional Dutch windmill in the country.

This windmill is the most popular part of the island, but you'll also find an extensive garden space here. You'll notice a few Dutch canals around the area, and there is an antique carousel in the middle of the park. A small village exhibit is also on display here.

Best Time to Visit: Windmill Island is open from April to October. Early May is the most popular time for the venue when the Tulip Time Festival is taking place.

Pass/Permit/Fees: Admission is $10 for adults and $5 for children.

Closest City or Town: Holland

How to Get There: From Grand Rapids, go west on I-196, and take Exit 55 to Business 196. Continue west on Chicago Drive, which soon becomes 8th Street. Go north on Lincoln Avenue, and you'll reach the entrance. The Holland stop on the Amtrak Pere Marquette line is to the south.

GPS Coordinates: 42.79949° N, 86.09590° W

Did You Know? You'll find more than 100,000 tulips on the island during the annual Tulip Time Festival.

Porcupine Mountains

You'll find the Porcupine Mountains in Gogebic and Ontonagon counties in the northwestern end of Michigan's Upper Peninsula. The mountains feature some of the oldest hardwood trees in the country. They also include an extensive basalt cliff that runs parallel to Lake Superior to the north.

You will find many sugar maple, yellow birch, and American basswood trees as you hike through the mountains. The mountains are also easy to climb, as they are close to 1,400 feet in elevation at their highest points.

Best Time to Visit: Conditions may be difficult during the winter, as the area is subject to lake-effect snow throughout the season.

Pass/Permit/Fees: You can visit the mountains for free.

Closest City or Town: Ironwood

How to Get There: From Ironwood, take US-2 east and then go north on County Highway 519. Go east on South Boundary Road to reach the mountains.

GPS Coordinates: 46.77968° N, 89.73413° W

Did You Know? The Porcupine Mountains get their name from the Ojibwa people who once lived here. They saw the silhouette of the mountains as a porcupine.

Henderson Castle

The Henderson Castle is one of the most beautiful houses in Kalamazoo. It is a bed and breakfast hotel dating to 1895.

The castle features a unique design with Lake Superior sandstone and brick around its body. The inside features 12 separate hotel rooms, each decorated in luxurious Victorian-inspired décor and accents.

The castle houses a winery, where it prepares various wines on site. There is also a steakhouse and spirits bar.

Best Time to Visit: The castle is open for reservations throughout the year.

Pass/Permit/Fees: You can book a room at the castle for $129 or more per night. You can also visit during the day, with tours available for $13 per person.

Closest City or Town: Kalamazoo

How to Get There: The castle is off of Main Street in western Kalamazoo. Main Street is accessible from the west on I-131.

GPS Coordinates: 42.29306° N, 85.60506° W

Did You Know? Michigan state law says that people cannot bring alcohol on the premises of a hotel. All alcohol purchases must be on site.

Kalamazoo Valley Museum

Kids will find plenty of fun things to explore at the Kalamazoo Valley Museum in downtown Kalamazoo. The hands-on museum has many exhibits dedicated to local art and science. There is also an exhibit highlighting the many items and products made in Kalamazoo.

The most popular part of the museum is an approximately 2,300-year-old Egyptian mummy that was donated to the museum in 1928. The exhibit dedicated to the mummy has features on carbon dating, CT scans, and forensic studies used to learn more about its origins.

Best Time to Visit: The museum is open year round.

Pass/Permit/Fees: Admission to the museum is free, although reservations for a visit are strongly encouraged.

Closest City or Town: Kalamazoo

How to Get There: The museum is on the North Kalamazoo Mall. You will find it north of the Arcadia Creek. You can reach the museum via Rose Street, which is between the west-moving Kalamazoo Avenue and the east-moving Michigan Avenue in downtown Kalamazoo.

GPS Coordinates: 42.29341° N, 85.58366° W

Did You Know? Some authentic guitars from Gibson are on display at the museum. Gibson was formed in Kalamazoo in 1902 and remains one of the world's top guitar developers and designers.

Canyon Falls and Gorge

The Canyon Falls and Gorge features a waterfall with a 30-foot drop. The waterfall is near the Sturgeon River in the Upper Peninsula and flows over black rocks, entering a nearby box canyon.

You'll also find many beautiful rock formations and indentations around the gorge leading to the waterfall. The formations have given the Canyon Falls area the nickname "Grand Canyon of the UP."

Best Time to Visit: You'll be able to see the natural colors of the area better during the spring and summer seasons.

Pass/Permit/Fees: You can enter the area for free.

Closest City or Town: L'Anse

How to Get There: The waterfall is about 7 miles south of L'Anse. Take US-41 south to reach the Canyon Falls Roadside Park area. There will be parking spots around the area north of the Sturgeon River. You can then take the North County Trail route south toward the waterfall.

GPS Coordinates: 46.62364° N, 88.47603° W

Did You Know? The dirt and black materials from the nearby rocks produce a distinct brown tone in the water in some parts of the area.

Sturgeon Falls

The northeastern end of the Ottawa National Forest is home to Sturgeon Falls. The waterfall features a height of about 25 feet with a crest of around 50 feet.

The waterfall comes from the Sturgeon River, a river formed from a gorge that goes hundreds of feet deep in some spots. The waterfall narrows as the water goes through, producing a misting effect that sprays in all directions.

Best Time to Visit: Like with other spaces around the Upper Peninsula, it may be tough to reach the space during the winter months.

Pass/Permit/Fees: The waterfall is open to visitors for free.

Closest City or Town: L'Anse

How to Get There: Take US-41 northwest from L'Anse to Baraga, then go west on US-38. Take Baraga Plains Road south, then go west of Clear Creek to reach Bears Den Overlook. You can find a few shots of the waterfall to the west from here.

GPS Coordinates: 46.64296° N, 88.69428° W

Did You Know? You will find various unspoiled red-rock formations in the cliffs on the gorge leading to the waterfall.

9-11-2001 Remembrance Memorial

The 9-11 Remembrance Memorial in Lansing pays tribute to the people who died during the 2001 terror attacks against the United States. The memorial includes a 10-foot H-beam that was gathered from the remains of the World Trade Center in New York. The beam features multiple twists and cracks, which it sustained during the attack. The memorial is located in the middle of a park area a few blocks east of the Michigan State Capitol. It is on the shore of the Grand River near the Rotary Steam Clock.

Best Time to Visit: The city of Lansing hosts a 9-11 remembrance event near the memorial on the anniversary of the attack each year.

Pass/Permit/Fees: The memorial is free to visit.

Closest City or Town: Lansing

How to Get There: Proceed north from the Grand Avenue exit on I-496. The memorial is in Wentworth Park past the Michigan Avenue bridge. CATA bus routes 1, 3, 8, 9, 10, and 11 all go through the area.

GPS Coordinates: 42.73403° N, 84.55028° W

Did You Know? The metal H-beam of the memorial gets its name from the H-shape it featured during its original construction.

Fenner Nature Center

Fenner Nature Center in Lansing is east of the Red Cedar River and Sycamore Creek. The 130-acre center features multiple self-guided trails where you can see many native trees from around the state.

The Monarch House is one of the most popular parts of the nature center. The structure features many monarch butterflies flying around. You can learn about the eight stages of a butterfly's life here.

The Davis Nature Pavilion hosts art galleries and nature exhibits throughout the year. The pavilion also offers educational programs about Michigan's unique ecosystem.

Best Time to Visit: The nature center is mostly outdoors, so the summer would be a good time to visit the area.

Pass/Permit/Fees: The center does not charge anything for admission, but donations are strongly encouraged.

Closest City or Town: Lansing

How to Get There: The center is directly west of the Michigan State University campus. Take Mount Hope Road from MSU's campus to reach the center. You can also reach Mount Hope Road from downtown Lansing by going south from I-496.

GPS Coordinates: 42.71257° N, 84.52303° W

Did You Know? The nature center is near the Potter Park Zoo in southeastern Lansing.

Hawk Island Park

Hawk Island Park in Lansing features 100 acres of park space for year-round activities. There is a swimming beach, plus multiple spots for picnics. There are about 1.5 miles of paved walkways that go around the park. You'll also find a few fishing docks throughout the area.

Hawk Island Park houses snow-tubing activities during the winter season. Cross-country skiing is open on the walkways when there is enough snow.

The park is also near the Soldan Dog Park, and there is an off-leash area with enough room for dogs to roam toward the northeast.

Best Time to Visit: The conditions here are best during the summer months.

Pass/Permit/Fees: The park does not charge admission for entry.

Closest City or Town: Lansing

How to Get There: The main entrance to the park is from the south on Cavanaugh Road. You can reach the park from I-496 by going west on the Dunckel Road exit and then turning right on Cavanaugh Road, continuing west until you reach the park.

GPS Coordinates: 42.69252° N, 84.52988° W

Did You Know? Part of the park is on the old Sablain Gravel Pit location. The old pit has a few planting areas where various native plants appear.

Impression 5 Science Center

The Impression 5 Science Center in Lansing takes its name from the five human senses. The venue features various educational play exhibits, where kids can learn all about the world around them. The center has hands-on exhibits about many things like how bubbles are formed and how water flows. There is also a spot for children up to four years of age called the First Impression Room where kids can experience various natural wonders and materials for the first time. The Think Tank is a teen-oriented space where kids use real tools to complete various science-based challenges. The Think Tank follows all STEM guidelines for education.

Best Time to Visit: Visit the website to learn about whatever traveling exhibits or attractions are at the center. The venue regularly changes out its exhibits.

Pass/Permit/Fees: Admission is $8.50 per person.

Closest City or Town: Lansing

How to Get There: Take East Michigan Avenue from the east to Museum Drive just before the Grand River. Go south on Museum Drive to reach the center. It's located a few blocks east of the Michigan State Capitol building.

GPS Coordinates: 42.73258° N, 84.54863° W

Did You Know? The center offers sensory-friendly hours for kids with sensitivity to external stimuli. Some of the exhibits are altered to keep sounds and other stimuli from being an issue.

Lansing Community College Sculpture Walk

Lansing Community College is home to a sculpture walk featuring dozens of sculptures in an outdoor environment. You will find many unique pieces around the park, including the 30-foot-tall *Red Ribbon in the Sky*. The ribbon is symbolic of the community college's link with the city's business district.

Other features around the sculpture walk include ones that represent construction, literature, and sailing. The Remembrance Memorial here holds a piece of steel salvaged from the World Trade Center in New York. You'll also find a typewriter-inspired sculpture and an art piece featuring two separate guitar players performing.

Best Time to Visit: The campus and its sculpture walk are open to visit during the daytime.

Pass/Permit/Fees: You can reach the walkway for free.

Closest City or Town: Lansing

How to Get There: The sculpture park is on Grand Avenue and starts in the middle of the LCC campus. You can reach the start north of Shiawassee Street in downtown Lansing. You can reach the area south from M-43.

GPS Coordinates: 42.73799° N, 84.55065° W

Did You Know? Some of the sculptures go down to the Michigan State Capitol building. This includes one sculpture of former state governor Austin Blair.

Meridian Historical Village

Take a trip back in time at the Meridian Historical Village in the eastern Lansing suburb of Okemos. The village features various nineteenth-century buildings perfectly restored to illustrate the history of the state. The buildings include a barn, schoolhouse, general store, and a log cabin.

The village houses a farmhouse dating to the 1860s. The Greek Revival building features a parents' bedroom, a children's room, and a weaving room.

Best Time to Visit: The village hosts a day camp in the summer where participants can see live reenactments of what people would do in the village during the 1860s.

Pass/Permit/Fees: The village is free to visit, although donations are encouraged.

Closest City or Town: Lansing

How to Get There: The village is north of M-43 east of Lansing. Go north on Marsh Road from M-43 and then turn left on Central Park Drive.

GPS Coordinates: 42.72868° N, 84.41493° W

Did You Know? A renovation project from a few years ago revealed a bunch of newspapers from the 1860s that were used as insulation underneath wallpaper for the farmhouse.

Michigan History Museum

Explore the story of Michigan at the Michigan History Museum, located a few blocks west of the State Capitol in Lansing. The museum houses exhibits on the story of the state, including a look at the Anishinaabe, the first native group to live in the area. The five-story building includes exhibits on the formation of the state, how it got its borders, and the Michigan industrial revolution of the twentieth century.

You'll find a white pine in the middle part of the building. The tree is emblematic of the distinct natural scenes throughout the state.

Best Time to Visit: The museum hosts multiple special exhibits during the year, including many about specific aspects of the state. The exhibits will vary based on what is open.

Pass/Permit/Fees: Admission is $8 for adults and $6 for children.

Closest City or Town: Lansing

How to Get There: The museum is on West Kalamazoo Street in downtown Lansing. It is north of I-496 between the Walnut Street and Martin Luther King Jr. Boulevard exits. CATA bus route 9 goes by the museum.

GPS Coordinates: 42.73200° N, 84.56291° W

Did You Know? You'll find a two-story relief map of Michigan on the second floor.

Michigan State Capitol

The Michigan State Capitol building in Lansing has been the home of the state legislature and the offices of the governor and lieutenant governor of Michigan since 1872. The Neoclassical building features a dome rising nearly 260 feet high. The inside of the dome features paintings of the eight Greek muses. The House chamber is loosely inspired by the United States Capitol chamber and has a ceiling with tiles featuring the coat of arms of each state. The Senate chamber has a walnut rostrum at the front where the lieutenant governor presides.

Best Time to Visit: Tours of the capitol are available. You can visit the chambers and the restored governor's office.

Pass/Permit/Fees: Tours are free, but reservations are encouraged.

Closest City or Town: Lansing

How to Get There: Exit onto East Michigan Avenue from US-43 to the east and then continue west on the road. East Michigan Avenue will eventually lead to the capitol across the Grand River. From the south, take the Pine Street exit on I-496 from Malcolm X Street. Go north on Pine Street, then turn right on Allegan Street. CATA bus routes 1, 3, 8, 11, 13, and 16 also serve the area.

GPS Coordinates: 42.73364° N, 84.55539° W

Did You Know? Lansing has served as the state's capital since 1847. The original capital was in Detroit, but it was moved to Lansing to help develop the western end of the state.

Michigan Women's Historical Center & Hall of Fame

The Michigan Women's Historical Center in Lansing highlights the many women who have made Michigan one of the country's greatest states. The "her-story" museum explains the many efforts women have made to improve equality and social justice throughout the state.

The center houses a hall of fame showcasing many of the women who have made a difference in Michigan history. This includes many trailblazers in the business industry.

Best Time to Visit: Walk-in tours are available on Tuesday and Thursday. You'll need an appointment during any other time of the week.

Pass/Permit/Fees: The museum is free to visit.

Closest City or Town: Lansing

How to Get There: The museum is on Allegan Street half a block west of the State Capitol. Allegan Street goes one way to the east. Take the Walnut Street or Martin Luther King Jr. Boulevard exit off of I-496 from the south or off of Business I-69 from the north to reach the museum. CATA bus route 48 also has a station nearby.

GPS Coordinates: 42.73249° N, 84.55270° W

Did You Know? The museum is a part of the Michigan Women Forward program, a state-run initiative that offers grants, scholarships, and other forms of support for women throughout the state.

Potter Park Zoo

Potter Park Zoo in Lansing is the oldest public zoo in Michigan. Formed in 1915, it houses more than 500 animals from about 150 species.

You will find Siberian tigers, African lions, and snow leopards at the zoo. It also has a bird habitat featuring exotic macaws, kookaburras, eastern screech owls, and cockatiels. Zookeepers hold classes in the summer months where visitors can learn more about how the animals are cared for and what the zoo workers do to help them.

Best Time to Visit: The zoo hosts its annual Wonderland of Lights festival in November and December.

Pass/Permit/Fees: Tickets are $14 for adults and $10 for children.

Closest City or Town: Lansing

How to Get There: The zoo is north of Red Cedar River. Take the Pennsylvania Avenue exit off of I-496 and go south, taking a left on Potter Park Road.

GPS Coordinates: 42.71797° N, 84.52763° W

Did You Know? Michigan State University provides medical care for the animals here. The university's College of Veterinary Medicine has a partnership with the zoo to support the well-being of the animals.

R.E. Olds Transportation Museum

The R. E. Olds Transportation Museum in Lansing is an automobile museum that houses many classic motor vehicles. The museum focuses on Oldsmobile and REO vehicles. The venue is named after Ransom E. Olds, the founder of Oldsmobile. The museum features an 1886 steam carriage that Olds designed himself. You'll also find one of the first Oldsmobile vehicles produced in 1897. There are dozens of Oldsmobile and REO vehicles on display dating back to 1897 through the end of the Oldsmobile line in 2004. A 1953 stock car used in NASCAR races is on display here. A 1996 GM EV1 electric vehicle is one of the newer vehicles you will find.

Best Time to Visit: The museum is open year round, but the museum encourages you to call ahead to see if a car that interests you is on display. The collection rotates throughout the year.

Pass/Permit/Fees: Admission is $10 per adult and $7 for children.

Closest City or Town: Lansing

How to Get There: Take Michigan Avenue east from US-127, then turn left on Museum Drive. You can also access it from the south by taking I-496 and going north on the Larch Street exit. From there, go left on Michigan Avenue and left on Museum Drive.

GPS Coordinates: 42.73132° N, 84.54768° W

Did You Know? The museum has a fully functioning half-scale replica of a 1906 REO vehicle.

The Michigan Princess

The *Michigan Princess* is a replica of a nineteenth-century steamboat. The boat is docked at the Grand River in Lansing.

The *Michigan Princess* offers three decks of entertainment. The first deck has a bar and dance floor. The second deck features 15 brass chandeliers and a scenic promenade. The third floor has a wheelhouse and provides the best outdoor views of the river.

Best Time to Visit: Cruises are available from March to December. Events also occur outside that timeframe, but the boat remains docked.

Pass/Permit/Fees: The price will vary by event. A lunch cruise or afternoon dinner cruise costs $51 per adult, while some specialty cruises like the Murder Mystery Dinner Cruise can cost $75 per person.

Closest City or Town: Lansing

How to Get There: The ship is off of Main Street in southwestern Lansing. Take the Waverly Road exit off of I-496 and go south, then go east on Lansing Road. The route will become Main Street not long after that.

GPS Coordinates: 42.72170° N, 84.58747° W

Did You Know? A typical lunch or dinner on the cruise will include at least three courses. You'll enjoy various meat and vegetable dishes along with a few sides to go with your meal.

Turner-Dodge House & Heritage Center

Visit the Turner-Dodge House & Heritage Center while in Lansing, and you will find one of the most historic places in the state. The 1858 house features a Classical Revival style with an outstanding look. You'll notice the Ionic columns throughout the venue and many rooms that have been refurbished to their original nineteenth-century styles.

The house also has a heritage center that holds multiple events throughout the year. These include art shows and other cultural programs.

Best Time to Visit: The holiday season is a popular time to visit, as the house is decked out with many lights and other accents.

Pass/Permit/Fees: Admission is $5 per person.

Closest City or Town: Lansing

How to Get There: The house is north of the Grand River. Take Larch Street north from Saginaw Street or Oakland Avenue, then move left on North Street to reach the house.

GPS Coordinates: 42.75108° N, 84.55208° W

Did You Know? The house is one of Lansing's most popular sites for weddings.

Arch Rock

Arch Rock is set on the eastern end of Mackinac Island. The limestone arch is a rare formation that stands about 146 feet above Lake Huron. Native Americans considered the arch to be a religious site. It was also critical to the formation of the Mackinac Island State Park, where you can travel multiple trails by bicycle or on foot.

Best Time to Visit: It is easier to see the natural formation during the daytime hours.

Pass/Permit/Fees: You can visit the arch for free but expect to pay at least $20 for a round-trip ferry ride to the island.

Closest City or Town: Mackinac Island

How to Get There: Take a ferry to the southern end of the island from Mackinaw City or St. Ignace, then hike about 1.3 miles from the ferry station to the northeast. The elevation rises by about 100 feet along the way. You can also take Lake Shore Drive or M-185 to the arch, but you will require a bicycle or horse to get there from the road since motorized vehicles are prohibited on the island.

GPS Coordinates: 45.85780° N, 84.60663° W

Did You Know? The arch is easy to spot from the east and west. You can see it downward toward the road and the shore from the west, or upward from the east.

Fort Mackinac

Fort Mackinac is a 1780 military outpost on the southern end of Mackinac Island near the main ferry port. The fort houses fourteen buildings that illustrate military life on the island in the nineteenth century.

You will see a few blockhouses on the grounds, plus the quarters for some of the residents who served here. There is also a guardhouse, a schoolhouse, and a soldiers' barracks.

The most popular part of the fort is its gun platform. The museum features a live cannon demonstration of how it is loaded and fired.

Best Time to Visit: The fort is open from June to October.

Pass/Permit/Fees: Admission is $13.50 for adults and $8 for children.

Closest City or Town: Mackinac Island

How to Get There: Take the ferry from Mackinaw City or St. Ignace, then go right on Main Street. Take a left on Fort Street, and you will find the fort to the left. The area is accessible by foot.

GPS Coordinates: 45.85223° N, 84.61736° W

Did You Know? The fort houses a tea room that is open to visitors with paid admission. The tea room opened to raise funds for World War I veterans in 1918, and it continues to be a fundraising source for the local park area.

Mackinac Island

Mackinac Island is an island in between the two peninsulas that make up Michigan. The island is home to an old fort built by the British before the United States gained control following the War of 1812.

Mackinac Island features many limestone growths and formations throughout its body. Arch Rock, Sugar Loaf, and Devil's Kitchen are among the most popular formations on the island. The area is also a prominent site for finding migrating birds. The southern end of the island is home to many small restaurants and bed and breakfasts. You can reserve a horse-drawn carriage ride while on the island from this area.

Best Time to Visit: Most of the activities on the island occur during the summer months. The island may not be easily accessible in the winter.

Pass/Permit/Fees: It costs at least $20 per person to ride a ferry to get to the island. The cost for renting a bicycle or roller blades will vary by site.

Closest City or Town: Mackinaw City

How to Get There: Take a ferry from Mackinaw City or St. Ignace to reach the southern end of the island.

GPS Coordinates: 45.84941° N, 84.61717° W

Did You Know? Cars and other engine-powered vehicles are prohibited on the island. These vehicles have been banned since 1898 out of concern that these "horseless carriages" will scare the carriage horses on the island.

Mackinaw City Beach

The Mackinaw City Beach is on the northern tip of the Lower Peninsula in Mackinaw City, a short ferry ride from Mackinac Island. The beach is near the Mackinac Bridge that links the Lower Peninsula with the Upper Peninsula.

This beach features an 1889 lighthouse on the eastern end. The Colonial Michilimackinac fort near the west houses an eighteenth-century fort that is open for tours.

Best Time to Visit: The summer season is an ideal time, as the ferry services in the nearby area are more active around that point.

Pass/Permit/Fees: The beach is free to visit.

Closest City or Town: Mackinaw City

How to Get There: The beach is on the southern end of the Mackinac Bridge. Take Exit 339 on I-75 before the bridge to reach Mackinaw City, then go north on Nicolet Street or Louvigny Street to reach the beach area.

GPS Coordinates: 45.78777° N, 84.73381° W

Did You Know? The Mackinac Bridge near the beach is nearly 5 miles long, making it one of the world's longest suspension bridges.

Kitch-iti-Kipi

Kitch-iti-Kipi is a spring in Schoolcraft County in the Upper Peninsula. The name is an Ojibwe term for "big spring." Kitch-iti-Kipi is about 40 feet deep and 300 by 175 feet in size. The spring features fissures in the underwater limestone area that produce nearly 10,000 gallons of spring water every minute. The water is consistently at about 45° F. You'll notice a distinct green tone in the water all around the area. The raft in the middle of the spring provides a view of the fissures at the bottom.

Best Time to Visit: The spring is open for visits throughout the year.

Pass/Permit/Fees: You can reach the spring for free.

Closest City or Town: Manistique

How to Get There: The spring is near the town of Manistique to the south. Take US-2 west from Manistique, then go north on M-149, which soon turns left. Go right on County Road 455 and then back onto M-149 to reach the spring. The spring is near the northwestern part of Indian Lake.

GPS Coordinates: 46.00433° N, 86.38146° W

Did You Know? There are many Native American legends surrounding the spring. One belief is that if a maiden drops a bit of honey on a piece of birch bark and adds it to the spring, the chieftain who receives it from the maiden will fall in love.

Manistique Beach

Enjoy the sights and sounds of northern Lake Michigan on Manistique Beach in the town of the same name in Schoolcraft County. The beach features a small boardwalk that goes near the lake and a hiking trail to the west. The trail goes through Lakeview Park and will take you toward the Manistique River to the west of the city. You will also find a small defunct lighthouse near the end of the beach.

Best Time to Visit: The summer is the best time to visit, as conditions can be rough in the winter.

Pass/Permit/Fees: The beach is free to visit.

Closest City or Town: Manistique

How to Get There: The beach is on the eastern end of the town of Manistique. You can reach it off of US-2. The highway straddles the northern end of the beach area.

GPS Coordinates: 45.95349° N, 86.22584° W

Did You Know? Manistique is the only city in Schoolcraft County. The town hosts more than half of the nearly 8,000 people that call the county home.

Black Rocks

The Black Rocks of Presque Isle Park near Marquette are ideal for cliff jumping. The Black Rocks are a rock formation about 20 to 30 feet above Lake Superior. The cliffs feature a naturally dark color that adds a unique look to the tip of the park.

You will experience an amazing view of the lake from atop the rocks. The area also has plenty of climbing spots that make it easier for you to get down toward the lake or back to the top if you're jumping off a cliff.

Best Time to Visit: The summer season is the best time to go cliff jumping, as the water won't be as cold.

Pass/Permit/Fees: The area is free to visit, but be sure to bring warm clothes.

Closest City or Town: Marquette

How to Get There: The Black Rocks are north of Marquette, which you can access from US-41. Take Presque Isle Avenue north from Marquette, then go right on Hawley Street and north on Lake Shore Boulevard. Continue on the street as it becomes Peter White Drive. The Black Rocks are at the northern tip of the park.

GPS Coordinates: 46.59273° N, 87.38067° W

Did You Know? The area doesn't have a lifeguard on duty, so be sure to go cliff jumping with a group instead of by yourself. Avoid diving during the winter season.

Sugarloaf Mountain

You can see much of Lake Superior from atop Sugarloaf Mountain near Marquette. The mountain and park areas feature multiple hiking trails, with many of them leading to the main observation deck. You will see the lake and heavily forested areas around the mountain from atop this space. You'll be a little over 1,000 feet above sea level.

You can also see Hogback Mountain from the western end. Sugarloaf Mountain is slightly higher in elevation.

Best Time to Visit: You will be more likely to see the appealing green tones of the trees in the area during the summer months.

Pass/Permit/Fees: You can reach the mountain range for free.

Closest City or Town: Marquette

How to Get There: Go north of Presque Isle Avenue from downtown Marquette, then turn left on Hawley Street, which soon becomes Big Bay Road. Continue until you see the mountain area to the right.

GPS Coordinates: 46.60444° N, 87.45610° W

Did You Know? A stone monument dedicated to one of the Boy Scout troops that lays claim to being the first troop in existence is near the mountain area.

Wetmore Landing and Little Presque Isle

You can take a hiking trip between Wetmore Landing and Little Presque Isle while on the Upper Peninsula. The 3.6-mile trail is an easy hike that doesn't have much of an elevation gain as you travel.

You'll find the Hidden Beach while hiking along Lake Superior. The beach is mostly secluded and features a brown tone formed by tannins from some of the rocks in the area.

You'll find Little Presque Isle at the end of the trail. The island area provides exciting views of the nearby town of Marquette.

Best Time to Visit: The summer season has the best weather for a visit.

Pass/Permit/Fees: The trail is free to visit.

Closest City or Town: Marquette

How to Get There: The trailhead is north of Marquette. Go north on Presque Isle Avenue, then go left on Hawley Street, which becomes Big Bay Road. Continue down the road until you reach the Wetmore Landing area.

GPS Coordinates: 46.61719° N, 87.46472° W

Did You Know? The Little Presque Isle area has a few private beach spots.

Manistee River Trail

The Manistee River Trail is on the western end of the Hodenpyl Dam Pond in Manistee County. The trail is about 11 miles long and goes through the eastern bank of the Manistee River.

This trail features various forms of vegetation, from pine trees to damp swamps. A few spring-fed waterfalls are here as well. The Hodenpyl Dam appears on the eastern end.

Best Time to Visit: The trail is open year around.

Pass/Permit/Fees: You can visit for free.

Closest City or Town: Mesick

How to Get There: The trail is a few miles southwest of the town of Mesick. Take M-37 south from Mesick and go west on 26 Mile Road. Go right on Hodenpyl Road and continue north. The main parking area for the trail is on O'Rourke Road to the right near the water.

GPS Coordinates: 44.36205° N, 85.82200° W

Did You Know? Most of the trail is on the eastern part of the river, but there is a suspension bridge to the north that will bring you over the water.

Beaver Lake Loop

Birdwatching enthusiasts will find many birds on the Beaver Lake Loop. The loop circles Beaver Lake, located in the Upper Peninsula. The trail is about 9 miles long.

The trail is mostly wooded, and it includes multiple turns around the nearby Pictured Rocks National Lakeshore. Parts of the loop reach the shore of Lake Superior. There are also a few camping sites, including those at Lowney Creek, Beaver Creek, and Pine Bluff.

Best Time to Visit: You'll find more birds from May to October.

Pass/Permit/Fees: The trail is free to visit. You may need to reserve a camping space at one of the grounds if you wish to stay overnight.

Closest City or Town: Munising

How to Get There: Travel on M-28 to Munising, which is east of Marquette. Take H-58 East from Munising, then go left on Little Beaver Lake Road to reach the loop. It's about 20 miles to get from Munising to the loop.

GPS Coordinates: 46.54214° N, 86.35787° W

Did You Know? Bears can be found in various parts of the loop. The campsites have lock boxes so that campers can secure their food to ensure bears won't rummage through their belongings.

Chapel Falls

Chapel Falls is among the tallest waterfalls in the state. It flows about 60 feet down into the Chapel Lake near Munising. You'll come across a few small hills as you go across the waterfall area, and there are two viewing platforms.

You can reach the waterfall through a small trail leading from Chapel Beach to the north. The trail goes up to the Pictured Rocks National Lakeshore in the Upper Peninsula.

Best Time to Visit: The summer is a good time to visit when the conditions will be more comfortable.

Pass/Permit/Fees: The waterfall is open to the public.

Closest City or Town: Munising

How to Get There: Take H-58 or Munising Avenue east from Munising. The road soon becomes Adams Trail, which goes through Van Meer and then north through Williams Crossing. Go left on Chapel Road to reach the Chapel Basin parking area. You can take a walking trail north from the entrance to the waterfall. You can also continue north to reach Chapel Beach.

GPS Coordinates: 46.52889° N, 86.44467° W

Did You Know? The water flows flat down the waterfall. The incline at the top provides a smooth surface that makes it easy for the water to flow downward.

Grand Island Loop

The Grand Island Loop is a 21-mile looping trail that goes through most of the perimeter of Grand Island in the Hiawatha National Forest. The trail starts at the ferry entrance at Williams Landing to the south.

The loop features a mostly gentle path, although it can rise by 200 to 300 feet in elevation depending on where you go. Backpacking is open here, and there are a few camping sites to the north. The 21-mile trail is ideal for mountain biking.

You will find the Grant Island North Lighthouse on the northern end of the loop. The lighthouse is situated on a massive cliff overlooking Lake Superior.

Best Time to Visit: The weather conditions are best in the summer.

Pass/Permit/Fees: It costs $5 to use the ferry to get to the island.

Closest City or Town: Munising

How to Get There: Take a ferry ride from Grand Island Lansing Road near Munising to reach the island. The road is off of M-28 north of Munising.

GPS Coordinates: 46.45595° N, 86.67550° W

Did You Know? While the loop is ideal for mountain biking, there are no paved roads on the island. You'll need to ensure that any bike you take can handle off-road conditions.

Miners Falls

The Pictured Rocks National Lakeshore in northern Alger County houses Miners Falls, a 40-foot waterfall around a sandstone outcrop. The waterfall features a 10-foot crest.

The waterfall is part of Miners River, which leads to Miners Lake and Miners Beach to the north. It is accessible from a half-mile gravel hiking path. You'll find a small lookout space near the end of the trail.

Best Time to Visit: The waterfall doesn't freeze during the winter season, so any time is good to visit.

Pass/Permit/Fees: You can reach the waterfall for free.

Closest City or Town: Munising

How to Get There: From Munising, go east on Munising Avenue, which becomes the Adams Trail, or H-58. Turn left on County Highway, then go right on Miners Falls Road. It is about 10 miles from Munising.

GPS Coordinates: 46.47509° N, 86.53095° W

Did You Know? Some parts of the Miners River near the waterfall are open for fishing, although you'll need a license to fish in Michigan.

Mosquito Falls

Mosquito Falls is a waterfall in the Upper Peninsula that links to a small beach overlooking Lake Superior to the north. The waterfall features two drops about 100 meters apart. The first drop is about 5 feet, while the second drop is 10 feet. It also features a 25-foot crest.

You'll reach the waterfall from the beach to the north. The beach is about 1.5 miles from the waterfall and is part of the Pictured Rocks National Lakeshore.

Best Time to Visit: The weather conditions are easier to manage during the summer season.

Pass/Permit/Fees: The area is free to visit.

Closest City or Town: Munising

How to Get There: The waterfall and beach are about 20 miles northeast of Munising. Take the Adams Trail H-58 east from Munising, then go left on Chapel Drive. Turn left on Camp Road or Route 695, and continue north on 695 until you reach the Chapel Basin parking area. The waterfall is about 1 mile west from the parking space.

GPS Coordinates: 46.51645° N, 86.47793° W

Did You Know? Most of the flowers in the area will bloom during the spring season. Some of these flowers will border the ends of the rapids.

Pictured Rocks National Lakeshore

You will find nearly 40 miles of lakeshore on Lake Superior at the Pictured Rocks National Lakeshore. Many of the beaches around the lakeshore surround the sandstone cliffs near the water. The cliffs are named for their multiple colors.

There are many white birch trees in the forests surrounding the lakeshore. The eastern part of the shore houses the Au Sable Light Station, an old lighthouse where you can see a few remnants of old shipwrecks in the area.

Best Time to Visit: The area is safer to visit during the summer, as there won't be immense amounts of snow in the area during that season.

Pass/Permit/Fees: You can reach the area for free, although it costs extra to reserve a campsite in one of the areas.

Closest City or Town: Munising

How to Get There: You can reach the lakeshore off of H-58 between Munising and Grand Marais. There are multiple parking areas around some of the campgrounds near the lake, including the Hurricane River Campground south of the Au Sable Light Station.

GPS Coordinates: 46.64530° N, 86.20704° W

Did You Know? The warmest waters are closer to Munising. The water can get up to 60°F or higher during the summer.

New Buffalo Beach

The southwestern end of the Lower Peninsula is home to New Buffalo Beach, overlooking the southern end of Lake Michigan. The beach features about 800 feet of shore. You'll find many opportunities for swimming, but the area also features an extensive marina for boats. The beach is part of a recreational area spreading through the town. It includes many surf shops and dining spaces on Whittaker Street.

Best Time to Visit: Most of the stores and other businesses in the area are open in the summer. Some places may close for the winter.

Pass/Permit/Fees: It is free to visit the beach, but it costs $15 to $20 to park between April and October. Parking is free during the off-season. Kayak and paddleboard rentals are available, but those cost extra.

Closest City or Town: New Buffalo

How to Get There: Take I-94 to reach New Buffalo. Go north on the Harbor County Drive exit a few miles past the state border. The road will become Whittaker Street, which will lead you directly to the middle of the beach. The Amtrak Wolverine and Blue Water routes have a station in the area.

GPS Coordinates: 41.80191° N, 86.74877° W

Did You Know? The beach is close to 60 miles away from Chicago. You can see a mirage of the Chicago skyline during the sunrise or sunset hours if the skies are clear enough.

Lake of the Clouds

You'll find a valley between two ridges of the Porcupine Mountains while in Ontonagon County in the Upper Peninsula. The Lake of the Clouds is inside the valley that divides the two main parts of the mountains. It's part of the Porcupine Mountains Wilderness State Park.

The lake is about130 acres in size and empties into Lake Superior to the north. It is surrounded by a vast forested area.

Best Time to Visit: The park often hosts nighttime sky-watching events at the lake, as the conditions are perfect for viewing the stars. These events are more likely to happen in the spring or summer.

Pass/Permit/Fees: You can reach the lake for free.

Closest City or Town: Ontonagon

How to Get There: You can get to the lake from Ontonagon by taking M-64 west and then continuing straight on the 107th Engineers Memorial Highway. You'll go past the visitor center and a skiing area before you reach the lake.

GPS Coordinates: 46.80730° N, 89.73971° W

Did You Know? The local area is surrounded by virgin wilderness. The term refers to a forest that has only been inhabited by indigenous people.

Great Lakes Shipwreck Museum

You will find artifacts from various shipwrecks at the Great Lakes Shipwreck Museum at Whitefish Point in Chippewa County. The museum houses items recovered from multiple ships, including several from the late nineteenth century, as well as a bell from the *SS Edmund Fitzgerald*.

The museum offers exhibits on the US Life-Saving Service and how it helped save people from various shipwrecks and marine emergencies. There is also a functioning lighthouse. You'll also find a steel lamp oil house from 1861 at the museum. A lookout tower is present, although it is not open to the public.

Best Time to Visit: The museum is open from May to October.

Pass/Permit/Fees: Admission is $14 for adults and $10 for children.

Closest City or Town: Paradise

How to Get There: From Sault Ste. Marie, take I-75 South and exit on M-28. Go west on the road, then take a north on M-123 near Strongs Corner. Continue north on Whitefish Point Road when you reach the town of Paradise. The museum is about 10 miles north of Paradise and about 70 miles from Sault Ste. Marie.

GPS Coordinates: 46.77113° N, 84.95766° W

Did You Know? The light tower that operates at the museum was built in 1861 and continues to be maintained today.

Tahquamenon Falls State Park

The Tahquamenon Falls State Park in Chippewa County features one of the largest waterfalls in the state. The Tahquamenon Falls has a 50-foot drop at the top and several smaller cascades leading down toward Whitefish Bay near Lake Superior. The waterfall also has a brownish color thanks to compounds from nearby cedar swamps that drain into the river.

You'll find more than 20 miles of hiking trails throughout the area. You can use a canoe or rowboat to reach the waterfall.

Best Time to Visit: The summer season is a comfortable time to visit the park.

Pass/Permit/Fees: Admission to the park is free. It costs extra to reserve one of the campsites here.

Closest City or Town: Paradise

How to Get There: The park is north of M-28 in the Upper Peninsula. Go north on US-123 from either Strongs Corner or Roberts Corner to reach the park.

GPS Coordinates: 46.60375° N, 85.20573° W

Did You Know? The river will drain up to 50,000 gallons of water in a second, making it the runner-up to Niagara Falls as the most voluminous waterfall east of the Mississippi River.

Bond Falls

Bond Falls is a waterfall in Ontonagon County in the Upper Peninsula. The waterfall has a drop of about 50 feet as the water moves from the Bond Falls Flowage north toward Lake Superior.

The waterfall is part of the Bond Falls Scenic Site. You will find multiple camping areas around the flowage site, but the main trails are near the waterfall on the northwestern end.

Best Time to Visit: You'll experience a picturesque look at the waterfall during the winter season. The water continues to flow even as the local conditions are freezing.

Pass/Permit/Fees: The waterfall is free to visit.

Closest City or Town: Paulding

How to Get There: The waterfall is near US-45, which goes north to Ontonagon and south to Eagle River, Wisconsin. Go east on Bond Falls Road in the town of Paulding, and continue following that road until you reach the waterfall.

GPS Coordinates: 46.40997° N, 89.13248° W

Did You Know? The waterfall was artificially produced by a dam from the Upper Peninsula Power Company. The dam helps produce enough energy for people throughout the Upper Peninsula.

Potawatomi Trail

The Potawatomi Trail is about 17.4 miles long and travels along many lakes in the area. You will find Halfmoon Lake to the southwest and the Crooked Lake to the southeast. Beaver and Gosling Lakes are to the north.

The trail goes through many forested areas near the towns of Hell and Chalkerville. Most of the camping sites around the trail are on the western end of the space.

Best Time to Visit: The trail is the easiest to travel from April to November.

Pass/Permit/Fees: You can reach the trail for free.

Closest City or Town: Pinckney

How to Get There: Take Patterson Lake Road, or D32, from Pinckney to the east or Stockbridge to the west to reach the trail.

GPS Coordinates: 42.42918° N, 83.99934° W

Did You Know? While Pinckney is the nearest major town to the trail, you can also find the town of Hell a little closer to the entrance. Hell is famous for its unusual name, which is believed to come from the German word for "bright."

Turnip Rock

Turnip Rock is one of the most unique geological sites to see in Michigan. The rock is a sea stack in the northeastern Lower Peninsula, specifically on the thumb portion.

Turnip Rock is a massive rock formation produced over centuries of wave action. The cross section is larger than the base, forming a pedestal-like design. The rock features a turnip shape, which gives the formation its name.

Best Time to Visit: The rock is open throughout the year.

Pass/Permit/Fees: It costs extra to reserve a boat that will take you up to Turnip Rock from Port Austin. Check with a charter service to see what it will cost to get there.

Closest City or Town: Port Austin

How to Get There: You can take a boat from Port Austin to reach the rock. Go north on M-53 from Detroit to reach the town.

GPS Coordinates: 44.06980° N, 82.95884° W

Did You Know? The rock features a concrete collar around its base near the waterline to prevent further undercutting, ensuring the structure will stay safe.

Ocqueoc Falls

In addition to being the Lower Peninsula's largest waterfall, Ocqueoc Falls is one of the country's few easily accessible waterfalls. You can reach the waterfall in Ocqueoc Township through a bike path, a hiking trail, or a nearby road.

Ocqueoc Falls features a flat design with the rapids flowing across multiple drops. The falls move through the Oqueoc River. The water is gentle enough that you can go swimming down the waterfall.

Best Time to Visit: The water is most comfortable during the summer season.

Pass/Permit/Fees: The waterfall is free to visit.

Closest City or Town: Rogers City

How to Get There: The waterfall is 12 miles west of Rogers City. Take M-68 West all the way from the city to the waterfall, taking a right on the fork to Ocqeoc Falls Highway.

GPS Coordinates: 45.39617° N, 84.05769° W

Did You Know? The trails around the waterfall are open for cross-country skiing during the winter months.

Soo Locks

The Soo Locks are a unique engineering marvel produced by the United States Army Corps of Engineers. The locks at Sault Ste. Marie are designed to help ships traveling on the St. Mary's River go between Lake Superior and Lake Huron. They were built in 1855 and continue to serve ships today.

There are two separate locks here. The first is the MacArthur Lock, which is about 80 feet wide. The second is the Poe Lock, which is 110 feet wide and can handle lake freighters. The Soo Locks are powered by a small hydroelectric plant. The plant produces enough energy to keep the complex operational.

Best Time to Visit: The spring and summer seasons are the peak times for ship operations at the locks.

Pass/Permit/Fees: You can visit the locks for free.

Closest City or Town: Sault Ste. Marie

How to Get There: You can observe the locks from a platform on West Portage Avenue in Sault Ste. Marie. Take the I-75 exit toward Lake Superior State University, then go east on Easterday Avenue and north on Ashmun Street. Take a left on Portage Avenue to reach the observation deck.

GPS Coordinates: 46.50233° N, 84.35100° W

Did You Know? There is a third lock on the Canadian side of the border, but that is for tour boats.

Warren Dunes Beach

The Warren Dunes Beach in the southeastern town of Sawyer is on nearly 2,000 acres of land overlooking Lake Michigan. The beach features about 3 miles of shoreline and 6 miles of trails for hiking.

The main dune at the beach rises to about 260 feet in height and provides outstanding views of the lake and various surroundings.

Best Time to Visit: The waters are their most comfortable during the summer, but you can visit the dunes throughout the year.

Pass/Permit/Fees: This attraction is free.

Closest City or Town: Sawyer

How to Get There: The dunes are off of I-94 near the Sawyer Road exit. Take the exit and go west, then head north on Red Arrow Highway to reach the campground.

GPS Coordinates: 41.91613° N, 86.60118° W

Did You Know? The Love Tree is one of the most noteworthy sights to see at the beach. The tree is actually a series of trees with their roots entangled together, most of which appear above the sand.

The Lost Peninsula

The Lost Peninsula in the far southeastern end of Michigan's Lower Peninsula is a small exclave formed in the 1830s following the Toledo War dispute. The land space is in Michigan, but it is separated from the rest of the state and can only be accessed by going through Ohio. The formation came after the state border was determined.

The Lost Peninsula is one of the state's most popular places for boating. You'll find a vast marina that links to North Maumee Bay. The area extends toward Lake Erie, and you can also find a few small islands nearby.

Best Time to Visit: The Lost Peninsula is open year round.

Pass/Permit/Fees: It is free to visit the Lost Peninsula, but it costs money to rent a boat.

Closest City or Town: Toledo, Ohio

How to Get There: From Detroit, take I-75 south and then take Exit 2 onto Summit Street. Continue south as you cross the state border into northern Toledo. Go left on 131st Street and left again on Edgewater Drive to reach the peninsula.

GPS Coordinates: 41.73361° N, 83.45988° W

Did You Know? The Lost Peninsula is an extension of the nearby town of Erie. About 140 people live on the peninsula.

Sleeping Bear Dunes National Lakeshore

You will find views more than 400 feet above Lake Michigan atop the dunes at the Sleeping Bear Dunes National Lakeshore. The lakeshore is in the northwestern part of the Lower Peninsula. You can climb up the dunes here to see the lake and the nearby North and South Manitou Island chain to the north.

The Platte River Point is a prominent beach in the area. Water from the nearby Glen Lake will flow into Lake Michigan from around here.

Best Time to Visit: The park area is open year round, although the weather conditions are most comfortable during the summer months.

Pass/Permit/Fees: You can reach the area for free.

Closest City or Town: Traverse City

How to Get There: The dunes are about 25 miles west of Traverse City. Take M-72 west from Traverse City to Empire, then go north on M-22, merging on M-109 to the left.

GPS Coordinates: 44.88583° N, 86.04712° W

Did You Know? You will find the remnants of a few nineteenth-century farmsteads while on some of the hiking trails in the area.

Ypsilanti Water Tower

The Ypsilanti Water Tower is a historic water tower on the southern end of the Eastern Michigan University campus in Ypsilanti. It opened in 1890 and features a distinct Queen Anne construction style. The tower is about 147 feet tall. It features a steel tank with a capacity of about 250,000 gallons. The tower also houses a bust of Demetrius Ypsilanti, a hero of the Greek War of Independence, with a Greek flag next to it.

This tower has become notorious for having a phallic-looking shape. It has become the most prominent building in town and is often used as a landmark for directions around the city.

Best Time to Visit: You can visit the tower at any point in the year.

Pass/Permit/Fees: The tower is free to visit, but you might not be able to enter the inside.

Closest City or Town: Ypsilanti

How to Get There: The tower is on West Cross Street. Take Washtenaw Avenue or M-17 east from US-23 to reach the tower on the southern end of EMU campus.

GPS Coordinates: 42.24591° N, 83.62456° W

Did You Know? The Joliet limestone brick design on the tower includes four crosses hidden in its layout. These crosses were built by the construction team with the belief that they would protect the workers from being hurt.

Proper Planning

With this guide, you are well on your way to properly planning a marvelous adventure. When you plan your travels, you should become familiar with the area, save any maps to your phone for access without internet, and bring plenty of water—especially during the summer months. Depending on the adventure you choose, you will also want to bring snacks and even a lunch. For younger children, you should do your research and find destinations that best suits your family's needs. Additionally, you should also plan when to get gas, local lodgings, and where to get food after you're finished. We've done our best to group these destinations based on nearby towns and cities to help make planning easier.

Dangerous Wildlife

There are several dangerous animals and insects you may encounter while hiking. With a good dose of caution and awareness, you can explore safely. Here is what you can do to keep yourself and your loved ones safe from dangerous flora and fauna while exploring:

- Keep to the established trails.
- Do not look under rocks, leaves, or sticks.
- Keep hands and feet out of small crawl spaces, bushes, covered areas, or crevices.
- Wear long sleeves and pants to keep arms and legs protected.
- Keep your distance should you encounter any dangerous wildlife or plants.

Limited Cell Service

Do not rely on cell service for navigation or emergencies. Always have a map with you and let someone know where you are and for how long you intend to be gone, just in case.

First Aid Information

Always travel with a first aid kit with you in case of emergencies.

Here are items to be certain to include in your primary first aid kit:

- Nitrile gloves
- Blister care products
- Band-aids - multiple sizes and waterproof type
- Ace wrap and athletic tape
- Alcohol wipes and antibiotic ointment
- Irrigation syringe
- Tweezers, nail clippers, trauma shears, safety pins
- Small Ziplock bags containing contaminated trash

It is recommended to also keep a secondary first aid kit, especially when hiking, for more serious injuries or medical emergencies. Items in this should include:

- Blood clotting sponges
- Sterile gauze pads
- Trauma pads
- Second-skin/burn treatment

- Triangular bandages/sling
- Butterfly strips
- Tincture of benzoin
- Medications (ibuprofen, acetaminophen, antihistamine, aspirin, etc.)
- Thermometer
- CPR mask
- Wilderness medicine handbook
- Antivenin

There is so much more to explore, but this is a great start.

For information on all national parks, visit: www.nps.gov.

This site will give you information on up-to-date entrance fees and how to purchase a park pass for unlimited access to national and state parks. This site will also introduce you to all of the trails of each park.

Always check before you travel to destinations to make sure there are no closures. Some hikes close when there is heavy rain or snow in the area, and other parks close parts of their land for the migration of wildlife. Attractions may change their hours or temporarily shut down for various reasons. Check the websites for the most up-to-date information.

Made in the USA
Middletown, DE
27 December 2022

20547257R00080